peas
and
thank
you

◆ HARLEQUIN®

peas and thank you

ISBN-13: 978-0-373-89240-2

Library of Congress Cataloging-in-Publication Data
Matheny, Sarah.

peas and thank you : simple meatless meals the whole family will love / Sarah Matheny.

p. cm.
Includes index.

ISBN 978-0-373-89240-2 (trade pbk.)
1. Vegetarian cooking. 2. Cooking, American. 3. Cookbooks. I. Title.
TX837.M394 2011
641.5'636—dc22
2010046174

Food photography by Ashley McLaughlin on pages xix (Pea Daddy photo), 42, 52, 66, 70, 74, 86, 90, 92, 95, 96, 108, 110, 140–141, 143, 158, 160, 180, 202, 210, 216, 218, 226, 228–229.

www.Harlequin.com

Printed in U.S.A.

To Gigi and Lulu,

the sweetest little Peas

a mama could ask for

peas
and
thank
you

Simple Meatless
Meals the Whole Family Will Love

Sarah Matheny

contents

Breakfast at the IHOP (International House of Peas)

1

Beyond Pea B and J: Lunches, Salads and Soups

Peas on the Side: Snacks, Sides and Sauces

Sure to "Peas" Dinners

4

Sweet Endings for Sweet Peas

5

acknowledgments

I AM SO THANKFUL.

I am thankful to God for blessing me with so many opportunities to love, laugh and learn in my life. "I can do all things through Christ who strengthens me" (Philippians 4:13).

I am thankful to my mom for always putting a book, a pencil and a whisk in my hand, and for telling me that I could be the pilot or the stewardess, because women can do anything.

I am thankful to my dad for listening to each and every crazy whim I got worked up about, from playing guitar to long-distance running to writing a cookbook. He always believed I would be the best at whatever I set my mind to, even if I didn't.

I am thankful to my grandparents, Kinky and Papa Bud and Amah Bobo and Papa Oscar, for teaching me about family and food and the beautiful memories that can be made when they intertwine.

I am thankful to my readers and fellow bloggers in the healthy-living blogosphere. You have inspired me with your creativity and encouraged me with your comments and support. Thank you for helping me find my voice and for being willing to "listen" to it every day.

I am thankful to my friends and neighbors for your help with the little Peas, putting up with my hectic schedule, accepting leftovers and offering feedback. Deb, Susan, Rachael, Angela and the Debban Family, you will always have a place at our table.

I am thankful to my friend and fellow foodie, Ashley McLaughlin for enhancing our project with snippets of her beautiful photography. You humored my crazy whim to be a part of this in the last hour and I will never forget those chaotic few days when we cooked, clicked, laughed and ate ourselves silly. You are forever an honorary Pea, like it or not.

I am thankful to my editor, Sarah Pelz, for helping craft my vision into reality, for putting up with rowdy background Peas on those long-distance calls and for getting (or at least *trying* to get) all of my silly jokes.

I am thankful to my agent, Lisa Grubka at Foundry Media, for putting my pitch in the "keep" pile, instead of turning it into scratch paper, and then for turning that pitch into the very strong foundation that has become this book. You took a chance on a silly, veggie stay-at-home mom, and in doing so, you changed my life.

I am thankful to Gigi and Lulu for having an infectious enthusiasm for life that has brought new meaning to mine. And for always being willing to take at least one bite of what I put on their plates. Or for spitting it into a napkin when I'm not looking.

I am thankful to Chris for saying "I do." Little did you know that meant unutilized law degrees, giving up meat, closets stuffed with more pink tutus than imaginable and the late night clicks of laptop keys. You are the best husband and daddy a Pea could have.

peas and thank you

introduction

I GREW UP IN YOUR AVERAGE AMERICAN HOUSEHOLD. WE ate cold cereal for breakfast, ham and cheese sandwiches and potato chips for lunch, pork chops and applesauce for dinner, and homemade chocolate chip cookies for dessert. It was a different time, and eating healthy meant adding just one teaspoon of sugar to a bowl of Honey Nut Cheerios, eating the crust in addition to the innards of a Wonder Bread sandwich, and drinking a large glass of milk to wash down that chocolate chip cookie.

I don't fault my parents for feeding me something close to the Standard American Diet. It was, after all, the standard. My mom was, and still is, an excellent cook, and with my chin eagerly perched on the kitchen counter, I watched in awe as she moved around our tiny kitchen. From my waist-high view, I learned how to slice vegetables with my fingers curled under, to not overmix my cake batter and that a canister of whipped cream makes excellent "Christmas trees" on an outstretched index finger. But of all the food lessons I learned from my family, the most important one was the value of eating dinner as a family almost every night. Sharing a meal that was lovingly prepared by my mother around a table with my brothers and my parents was more important than what was on our plates.

Even so, I made the connection early on in life that some choices are healthier than others. My dad was a smoker when I was born, and you can bet, as soon as Daddy's Little Girl figured out that they weren't called "cancer sticks" by chance, all it took were a few tears and an "I love you, Daddy" to change minds and hearts. My husband ("Pea Daddy") has had many similar experiences as a father, most often involving something pink, frilly or an impossibly small waist, blond hair, and feet that were just made for high heels. After my appeal to my dad that night, I awoke to find a carton of my father's cigarettes in the trash can. He never smoked again. This was my first lesson in the power of tears as a tool of manipulation, to be used less sincerely throughout my childhood and adult life. More important though, in that moment, seeing my dad's Marlboros sticking out of the can underneath the kitchen sink, I realized that parents aren't perfect and sometimes have to admit that they are wrong.

That lesson hit home in a different way many years later while having a snack with my daughter Gigi. She was happily munching on some orange wedges that were not-so-happily dripping down her face and onto her Gymboree shirt that I paid far too much for. As I sipped my third Diet Coke of the day and munched on a handful of Sweet 'n Salty Chex Mix, she did what all kids do and begged for what I had. I told her no, that soda and junk food were bad for her. I cringed when I thought of caffeine, aspartame and artificial coloring streaming through her tiny body. Suddenly it hit me: I was a hypocrite. I had a long talk with myself in hushed tones that night, poured out my diet soda cans and put them in the recycling bin. Then I finished the bag of Chex Mix and recycled the bag, too. (There was no point to just wasting food, right?) After that processed-food breakup, it wasn't long before my dietary choices moved on to even greener pastures.

I wouldn't necessarily call myself an animal lover. We had pets growing up, including a fox terrier who chewed his way through a gas barbecue hose, a hot water heater, a piece of plywood and a five-pound chocolate bar that he found under the tree on Christmas

Eve. Having your dog go into cardiac arrest kind of puts a damper on Christmas morning. I liked our dog okay, but lived in fear that he would do something to upset my dad, who after cleaning up the kitchen trash strewn all over the living room for the sixteenth time had nicknamed him "POSGE" (pronounced PAHS-JEE), an acronym for "Piece Of S*&# Garbage Eater."

When I started my own household, I wasn't in any big hurry to get a pet to destroy my things. That's what kids were for. And I certainly never intended to become a vegetarian, let alone a vegan. Until one night a friend sent me an email with a video of Sarah Palin visiting a turkey farm in her governor capacity to pardon a turkey for Thanksgiving. The irony of the video was that as the rogue politician declared one turkey free, another turkey was refusing to die (much like Ms. Palin's political aspirations) and was being violently slaughtered in the background. My stomach turned, my mouth dropped and tears sprang to my eyes. I'm not sure what dream world I was living in, but apparently I thought that Tinker Bell came and sprinkled magical sleeping fairy dust over live turkeys and they somehow ended up on a platter in my grandmother's dining room with a side of the most delicious mashed potatoes I would ever taste.

This violent and abrupt realization of where my food came from impacted my choices from then on. I read literature about factory farms and learned that the terrible conditions in most threaten the safety of our food. I decided I was no longer willing to eat meat. I started preparing more and more vegetarian meals for myself while continuing to serve up abnormally large breasts (the *only* abnormally large breasts in our house) to the family. Meanwhile, memories of my "jilted lover," Diet Coke, and ridding my life of its grasp came back to haunt me. I had banned aspartame and artificial flavorings for the household, but served daily meals of animal flesh washed in ammonia?

On a more practical level, my family missed seeing my face at the dinner table while I cooked up a steak for Pea Daddy, steak fries and nuggets for the girls, and a tofu steak for myself. After a few weeks of cooking three dinners a day, Pea Daddy surprised me by volunteering to follow my lead at dinnertime and become a vegetarian himself. I was thrilled. While his announcement wasn't an exhilarated "I'll have what she's having" moment out of *When Harry Met Sally*, once he saw that he could enjoy a meatless meal (and multiple times a day, at that), Pea Daddy was excited for all of us to make the transition to vegetarianism.

It wasn't long until Gigi asked why we were no longer eating chicken. I started to explain that it was important that we not hurt animals, and didn't she agree that we wouldn't want to hurt the chicken that we saw at local farmstand last weekend? "Not the kind of chicken that lives on a farm, Mama!" she scolded me. "The kind of chicken that you EAT!" I wasn't sure if I should hug her for being so naïve, or immediately put a helmet on her to prevent further brain injury. It was time to have "the talk," and I spent the next twenty awkward minutes acting out the most macabre scene to ever have been depicted using a Fisher Price Little People farm set. I'm afraid she still has nightmares about Farmer Jed.

From then on, it became my mission to transition my family from the Standard American Diet to something better, but I knew that I couldn't change who I was in making the transition. I wasn't going to make my own soap or sew our clothes. I can't even sew a button. I wasn't about to trade *The Bachelorette* and my flatiron for a PETA rally and dreadlocks. I'm too addicted to reality TV and straight hair for that. Though I enjoy a nice bowl of granola, I'm no "granola" mom, and I don't have to be "perfect" to lessen the environmental impact I have on the planet.

I want our foods to be fresh, organic when possible, meat-free and, for the most part, free of all animal products. But most important, our meals have to be delicious. I want my children and husband to come to the dinner table each night with the same feelings of excitement and anticipation that I had as a child, and to leave the dinner table with the same contentment and satisfaction. Ideally,

I still want to be the mom interested in the dinner conversation and not the food police interested in laying down the law.

Through trying new foods and recipes and having a sense of humor about the entire thing, we've done it. We've learned to respect animals by eating foods that have not gone through fear or pain, as the animals on factory farms do, but by enjoying delicious, plant-based recipes that keep every member of our family happy. In return, we've learned to love our bodies more and accept them the way they are. We appreciate them for the things they can do rather than what they look like. As a mother of girls, this is a lesson that is especially important to me.

We've also experienced the beneficial side effects of saving money and reducing waste. More important, we all have improved energy and overall health. We are sick less often and have more motivation to get up and out to play. We aren't "skinny bitches"; we're a fit, fun family, who enjoys life and what we eat. I want to make it easy for you to do the same.

This book is not going to try to label you as a vegetarian or a vegan or make you become one. Nor is its goal to make you feel guilty for those nights when you can't bear to cook and order a pizza instead. I'm just giving you another choice—simple plant-based versions of your family's favorite meals, most of which can be prepared and served in forty-five minutes or less. Take what you can from it, whether it's trying a new meat-free recipe once a week, or just reading the ridiculous stories about navigating life with two young girls, the days when the closest thing I get to a shower is a baby wipe and a fresh coat of deodorant, and when dinner is last night's leftovers. Again. But at least I know that those leftovers didn't have a mother, and I always serve them with a side of peas.

meet the peas

Mama Pea

Attorney turned stay-at-home mom, she's traded power lunches for tea parties, legal briefs for bedtime stories, and oral arguments for... well, oral arguments. She loves pop culture, worn-in yoga pants, bronzer and broccoli. She feels sleep is highly overrated. Same goes for cheeseburgers.

Pea Daddy

Attorney and the definition of "hands-on dad," Pea Daddy has four obsessions: root beer, island-themed kitsch, baseball and his girls. Mama Pea lumps herself into the "girls" category. She's nobody's "woman," but she'll always be Pea Daddy's girl.

Gigi

Dramatic five-year-old who was born to dance. She'll sing an off-key Taylor Swift song with reckless abandon and unrecognizable lyrics, then unapologetically declare, "I'm so beautiful, I could cry!" Just don't even think about trying to get her out of a skirt, dress or, more likely, tutu and into pants.

Lulu

Three-year-old cuddle buddy, alarm clock and Gigi protégé. She firmly believes that every recipe should include dill pickles, especially peanut butter sandwiches. A self-taught expert at giving the stink-eye, she reserves it for when Pea Daddy turns on baseball, Gigi sings or Mama Pea has the audacity to wash Blankie. Seriously, don't touch Blankie.

Pea Kitty

Seven-year-old furniture destroyer and former head of household. In a previous life she was a middle-aged clerk at a high-end retail store—she has the air about her that she thinks she is better than you, yet she is the one who is hocking up overpriced clothes made in China, or a hairball, as the case may be. To this day, Mama Pea interacts with Pea Kitty (and snobby clerks) only when she has to. Pea Kitty wants her dead. Not today, cat. Not today.

in the peas' pantry

THERE ARE FEW THINGS MORE FRUSTRATING TO ME THAN cracking open a new cookbook, flagging pages of enticing recipes I'd like to try and then realizing that not only do I not have some of the ingredients, but that I don't know what many of them are, let alone where to find them. I don't want that to happen to you with this book. You'd miss out on some delicious recipes, but even worse, you'd miss out on some great staples that I can't imagine cooking without or not eating. If you can't find these products in your local stores, look online or don't be afraid to ask your stores to carry them. The stores don't necessarily know what you want unless you tell them. That being said, here's a peek in our pantry.

AGAR AGAR: a vegan substitute for gelatin made from red algae. It can be found in flakes or sheets, but I find the powdered form to be easiest to find and the most economical. Look for it in the bulk foods section of your natural foods store or online.

AGAVE: also known as agave syrup or agave nectar, this sweetener comes from a cactus-like plant from Mexico. Agave is similar in sweetness and consistency to honey, but doesn't have the trademark honey flavor. It's fairly easy to find in most supermarkets, but you may also be able to buy it for less and in a smaller quantity in the bulk liquids section of your natural foods store.

ALMOND BUTTER: an alternative to peanut butter made from almonds. Growing in popularity, almond butter can be found in most supermarkets. Many natural foods stores also have machines that offer freshly ground varieties.

CHIPOTLE IN ADOBO SAUCE: canned smoked jalapeño chiles packed in a spicy tomato sauce. Found in the ethnic foods aisle of most supermarkets.

COCONUT MILK: not to be confused with coconut water (the actual liquid found inside the coconut), the milk is actually made from coconut meat. Most supermarkets carry both full fat and light varieties of coconut milk in the ethnic foods aisle, or you can find it at your natural foods store.

DARK CHOCOLATE CHIPS: chocolate in its purest form (cacao) doesn't contain milk sugar or a lot of additives. The darker the chocolate, the richer it is in antioxidants as well. Not all brands are dairy-free, but the higher quality brands are. If you don't care for dark chocolate (gasp!), look for organic, dairy-free chocolate chips at your supermarket or natural foods store.

FLAXSEEDS: seeds from the flax plant that are rich in fiber, protein and omega-3 fatty acids. In order to utilize the nutrients, flaxseeds must be ground before consuming, and so you may also come across "flax meal" and "ground flaxseed." However, I always grind my own to save cost and to keep the flax fresher longer. Store flaxseeds in the refrigerator to preserve their life. For egg-free baking, substitute 1 tablespoon of ground flax dissolved in 3 tablespoons of water for one egg. (A tablespoon is also an easy and indistinguishable addition for smoothies if any Peas are "backed up.") Flaxseeds can be found in the baking and cereal aisle or bulk section of your natural foods store.

HOISIN SAUCE: the Asian equivalent to barbecue sauce, it has a nice plum flavor that works great in stir-fries or dipping sauces. Look for it in the ethnic foods aisle of your supermarket.

LIQUID SMOKE: a flavoring made from vaporized smoke produced through burning wood chips. Highly potent, liquid smoke gives barbecue sauce its trademark flavor. You can find it next to the barbecue sauces in the condiment aisle of your supermarket.

MINCED GARLIC: garlic cloves that have been peeled, minced and packed into jars. This is one convenience ingredient that I always buy to keep my cloves from going bad and my fingers from getting stinky (or at least stinky because of garlic). Find the jars next to the garlic cloves in the produce section of your supermarket.

NON-DAIRY CHEESES: cheeses made from soy milk, almond milk or rice milk, these products vary greatly in flavor and quality. The cream of the crop in terms of flavor and texture is Daiya, a brand made without soy or casein (milk protein). At publication, Daiya is available only in shredded mozzarella and cheddar varieties, but the difference in quality more than makes up for a lack of variety. Daiya can be found at most Whole Foods and some other major supermarkets. Beware of other seemingly "non-dairy" varieties that have hidden casein in their ingredients list. Follow Your Heart is another casein-free brand that offers several other flavors. Look for non-dairy cheese in the refrigerated section of your natural foods store.

NON-DAIRY MILK: among the many varieties of non-dairy milk available are soy, almond, rice, oat and hemp. I like to switch up the varieties we use, using almond milk in most of our smoothies and on cereal and soy milk in baking. Pay attention to both the flavor (vanilla doesn't work well in savory recipes) and whether or not the milk is sweetened or unsweetened (some sweetened brands are packed with sugar). Most supermarkets offer soy, almond and rice milk, and all varieties can be found at your natural foods store, either in the refrigerated section or in shelf-stable packaging in the beverage aisles.

NUTRITIONAL YEAST: a nutritional supplement/condiment made from a deactivated yeast, "nooch" has a nutty, salty, cheesy flavor. It is high in vitamin B_{12} and protein, and is most definitely an acquired taste. We've acquired it…on popcorn, tofu, in dressings, et cetera. You can find it in the spice section of your natural foods store, or buy it for less and in a smaller (or larger, as the case may be) quantity in the bulk section.

ORGANICS: while not everything I buy is "organic" (produced free of synthetic materials, i.e., chemicals, pesticides, hormones or genetic modification), there are many items we buy that I won't buy otherwise. These are:

○ ORGANIC DAIRY PRODUCTS: though we primarily don't consume dairy products, occasionally the girls or Pea Daddy will eat organic sour cream, cheese, yogurt or ice cream. Ideally, organic dairy is made from milk produced by cows that are 1) fed organic grain; 2) raised in low-stress, healthier environments; and 3) not routinely given growth hormones or antibiotics. By choosing organic dairy, you will not just be giving your family a higher quality product, you will be supporting an industry that will preserve the environment and improve the quality of life for farm animals. Organic dairy is becoming cheaper and more commonplace every day, and the more consumers that demand organic dairy, the further prices will go down. Many supermarkets carry their own lines of organic dairy products and of course, you can find organic dairy products at natural foods stores.

○ **THE "DIRTY DOZEN" FRUITS AND VEGETABLES:** these produce purchases are those that the Environmental Working Group has named as most likely to have high pesticide residue if grown conventionally.

- Apples
- Bell peppers
- Blueberries
- Celery
- Cherries
- Grapes
- Kale
- Nectarines
- Peaches
- Potatoes
- Spinach
- Strawberries

I won't buy anything on this list for my family unless it is organic. I'd rather have my girls eat a conventional banana than a clump of non-organic grapes. A lot of supermarkets now offer organic produce, and if you watch for sales, many times you can buy organic items at the same price, if not cheaper, than their conventional counterparts. Trader Joe's and Whole Foods both offer extensive amounts of organic produce, and at Costco, you can often find industrial-sized offerings of organic produce, too.

QUINOA: an ancient Incan grain with a nutty flavor and an almost fluffy texture when cooked. Quinoa is high in protein and actually the only naturally occurring plant-based food that contains all nine essential amino acids. Your supermarket may carry quinoa next to rice and other grains, or you can find it in bulk or in the grains aisle of your natural foods store.

RED LENTILS: my favorite variety of lentil, the red lentil lacks the earthy aftertaste that is more common in the standard brown variety. Red lentils cook very quickly and become quite soft. Look for them next to beans and peas at your supermarket, or you are sure to find them in bulk or with other legumes at your natural foods store.

SEITAN: a virtually flavorless meat substitute made from wheat gluten, seitan is probably the closest in texture to chicken than any other faux meat on the market. You can buy flavored varieties or marinate it yourself. Seitan can be found in the refrigerated section of most natural foods stores.

SPROUTED GRAIN BREAD: a hearty bread made from sprouted whole grains, the most well-known variety of this flourless bread is Ezekiel 4:9 made by the Food for Life company. Sprouted grains retain their nutrients and natural plant enzymes, making this bread a nutrition powerhouse. Look for sprouted grain breads in the freezer case in your supermarket or natural foods store.

STEVIA: a natural sweetener made from the stevia plant, stevia has no calories, no effect on blood glucose and is up to three hundred times sweeter than sugar. We use stevia to sweeten our coffee and tea, in our oatmeal or to make a tart smoothie not so tart. Some stevia manufacturers, such as NuNaturals, offer a stevia baking blend that I use to substitute for the sugar in many cookie or cake recipes. You can find stevia in most supermarkets, though in some areas you may have to look in your natural foods store instead.

TAHINI: a paste made from ground sesame seeds, tahini gives hummus its distinct flavor. Tahini also makes delicious dressings and sauces. You can find tahini in most supermarkets and natural foods stores, next to the nut butters or in the ethnic foods aisle.

TEMPEH: a meat substitute made from fermented soybeans, tempeh is nutty, hearty and versatile. Like seitan and tofu, tempeh can be purchased in flavored varieties or you can marinate it yourself and then grill it, bake it, sauté it, et cetera, just like meat. Tempeh can be found in the refrigerated section of most natural foods stores. My favorite commercial tempeh preparation is Lightlife's tempeh bacon, Fakin' Bacon. It is delicious! You can also buy it in the refrigerated section of many natural foods stores.

TOFU: buckle up, here's your tofu crash course!

○ FIRM OR EXTRA-FIRM TOFU: these varieties come in water and are found in the refrigerated section of your grocery store. When you order tofu at a restaurant, this is the kind of tofu you'll get. If you drain and press this tofu, and then marinate it, you can grill it, bake it, sauté it, et cetera, just like meat. It has a dense, chewy texture, and personally, we love it.

○ HOW TO PRESS FIRM OR EXTRA-FIRM TOFU: you can buy a tofu press like the one made by TofuXpress. If you love tofu like we do, this is a great investment for your kitchen. If you don't want to shell out for a press, you can press the tofu yourself. Open the package, drain the tofu and then slice it into cubes or slabs. Line a breadboard with a clean tea towel or dish rag. Place tofu on top of the towel or rag, and then place another clean towel or dish rag on top of the tofu, followed by another breadboard. Stack numerous heavy objects (pans, books, children…) on top of the bread-board and let sit for anywhere from 20 minutes to 2 hours (the longer you press it, the firmer it will become). Prepare tofu as desired.

○ PRECOOKED TOFU: many natural foods stores offer prepared tofu in the refrigerator case next to the regular packages of tofu. These are often offered in several flavors, and obviously these have already been pressed, marinated and baked. While precooked tofu is often more expensive, and might have extra sodium that you might not have if you prepare it at home, it can be a great alternative if you are in a pinch.

○ SILKEN TOFU: also offered in firm or extra-firm varieties, this tofu has the moisture left in the soybean curd and isn't pressed at all. It has a silky texture, hence the ingenious name of silken tofu. I like to use it in smoothies, puddings and other desserts, but it can also be used as a binding agent in cooking or baking. It is shelf stable and doesn't have to be refrigerated. It can be found in the ethnic foods aisle of your supermarket or natural foods store, but it might also be offered in the refrigerator case.

VEGAN CREAM CHEESE: a non-dairy spread for use on bagels or toast, or in frostings, baked goods or savory recipes. Tofutti Better Than Cream Cheese is readily available in the refrigerator case of most natural foods stores, or Follow Your Heart also makes their own version.

VEGAN MARGARINE: a non-dairy spread for use on toast or for cooking, the most popular and readily available brand is Earth Balance. It is rich, buttery and simply delicious. Some commercial margarine spreads, like Smart Balance Light and Blue Bonnet Light are also vegan; however, while these products are fine as everyday spreads, they do not work well in baking cookies, pastries or other baked goods due to their high water content. Look for Earth Balance or other vegan margarines in the refrigerator case of most major grocery stores or in your natural foods store.

VEGAN MAYONNAISE: an egg-free, dairy-free spread for use on sandwiches or in dips and salad dressings, the most popular and readily available brand is Vegenaise. It offers a reduced-fat version and really does taste like traditional mayonnaise. Nasoya also offers a vegan mayonnaise, Nayonaise, which I find tastes more like Miracle Whip than mayo. Use whichever you prefer. You can find both in the condiment aisle of your natural foods store.

VEGAN WORCESTERSHIRE SAUCE: while traditional Worcestershire sauce contains anchovies, vegan varieties are meat- and dairy-free. Annie's Organics and The Wizard's both make vegan versions, or you may find that some organic brands are also anchovy-free.

Just make sure to check the label. Look for vegan Worcestershire sauce in the condiment aisle of your natural foods store.

WHOLE WHEAT PASTRY FLOUR: also known as white whole wheat flour, this flour has a lower gluten content and the light consistency of traditional all-purpose flour, but still has the bran and germ of whole wheat flour and thus all the nutritional benefits as well. The results are lighter, fluffier pancakes, muffins and cookies than those made with regular whole wheat flour. I try to use primarily whole wheat pastry flour in all my baked goods, but reserve using organic, unbleached all-purpose flour for rare treats. You may also find that your family prefers a combination of whole wheat pastry flour and unbleached flour while they transition from eating the white stuff. Just don't use whole wheat pastry flour, or at least not all whole wheat pastry flour, in breads or yeasty baked goods as it lacks the gluten to give your dough a good rise. Most supermarkets offer whole wheat pastry or white whole wheat flour in bags in the baking aisle, but I much prefer to buy it in bulk from the bins where it is airy and looser than the kind packed into the bagged "bricks."

Breakfast at the IHOP (International House of Peas)

1

BREAKFAST IS ONE DIVISIVE MEAL. THERE ARE TWO MAIN CAMPS OF thought regarding breakfast: those who eat it and those who don't. I am sheepish to admit that in my pre-child days, while I felt I needed bras that matched my underwear, pedicures and other such luxuries like daily showers, I never felt I needed breakfast. A cup of coffee and a smile got me through a morning of desk work just fine.

However, now I am one of the world's strongest proponents for breakfast. I could sit here and tell you that it's the most important meal of the day, and that the meaning of the word is to literally "break the fast," but what am I, your seventh-grade health teacher? I've simply learned that when my morning includes putting Gigi into a headlock so I can try to tame her curls with a squirt bottle and a comb, and keeping Lulu from playing treasure hunt in the litter box, a cup of coffee just isn't going to cut it. I need four cups. And some food. I'm not the only one who is just plain hungry when I wake up, either; I've barely got my contacts in before I hear little hands opening refrigerators and cupboards (yes, Pea Daddy has freakishly little hands).

That's where the second polarizing issue comes in—deciding what kind of breakfast there's time for and who's going to make it. Many factors weigh into this decision, including if it's a day where we're oh-so-happily driving the carpool across town or if I manage to resist the urge to pound the snooze button and actually get my workout in before we're all treated to Lulu's enigmatic crib version of "Twinkle, Twinkle Little Star." On those busy weekdays, we'll generally veer toward the smoothies, oatmeal or hot cereal that Pea Daddy can easily make while I chase Gigi with a can of hairspray. Other times I've thought ahead and made extra waffles, pancakes or scones for the week, so those go in the toaster while I wrestle a litter scoop away from Lulu. And on the weekends, we throw caution to the wind and make cinnamon rolls or French toast, even if it makes us slightly late for church.

I'm not going to harp on you about breakfast. I won't force you to look at "I Brake for Breakfast" stickers on my car or knock on your door with a pamphlet and petitions. The proof is in the pudding, and I have faith that once you try a few of these breakfast recipes, I'll have made a breakfast believer out of you, too.

blueberry streusel muffins (page 20)

blackberry basil smash smoothie

Makes 4 smoothies

IT'S NO SECRET THAT PEA DADDY IS A FAN OF TOMMY BAHAMA, ALSO known in our house as "The Old Man Store." He has a dozen or so Tommy Bahama shirts, two sets of Tommy Bahama coffee mugs, Tommy Bahama bed pillows and even Tommy Bahama cologne. It smells just like Grandpa. I love to tease him about it, and he likes to defend his favorite store by saying that it is young at heart, and its actual demographic is men aged thirty-five to sixty-five, to which I respond, "But you are only thirty-three!"

Sometimes, his unrequited affection for clothing of the elderly works to my advantage, like when he bought me a very nice Tommy Bahama dress for Valentine's Day, or when it inspires a new smoothie recipe.

On our vacation to Hawaii, Pea Daddy learned there was a Tommy Bahama restaurant on the Big Island. We immediately had to put in his dentures, change his Depend and hit the road, not exceeding thirty-five miles per hour, mind you. I think he felt a little guilty making us drive about thirty miles to visit the restaurant, but not nearly as guilty as when we got there at 3:00 p.m. and they didn't open until 4:00.

I'm not sure the Tommy Bahama folks were happy to have two toddler girls, their bikini-and-cutoffs-clad mom and a well-dressed, fine-smelling father loitering in their store for an hour, a fact that was worsened by Gigi suddenly remembering the phrase that I had taught her last time we went to a Tommy Bahama store, "Ew! It smells like old man in here!" They were even more thrilled when we parked ourselves in the waiting area until they opened.

It wasn't long before Lulu was having a fit because she wanted to ride the elevator up and down, and the rest of the waiting patrons had seen which pair of Princess panties Gigi was wearing as she sat on the Hawaiian-patterned couch like a four-year-old Britney Spears. I turned to Pea Daddy and said, "Listen, Gramps, this had better be worth it!" To which he said, "What? Speak up! My hearing aid's at the condo."

When the restaurant opened, they led us as far away from human life as possible and parked us in a booth in the bar. That's right, Baby's First Happy

Hour! To my surprise, they had a Kids' Menu, but the girls weren't really down with Chicken Fingers and Mini Sliders, so we ordered an adult's Strawberry Smoothie for them to share. While waiting for her smoothie, Lulu used her crayons to color on the table, and when her drink came, she intentionally dumped half on the table. You owe me $5.50, kid. That smoothie cost $11.00, and Daddy's social security check hasn't come yet.

It should come as no surprise that I was strongly considering ordering an adult beverage. One particular drink caught my eye because of the interesting flavor combinations. And the rum. I didn't order the Blackberry Basil Smash, but it sounded intriguing, with its mix of rum, sour mix, basil, blackberries and soda. Since I can't drink rum for breakfast, I decided to make a smoothie version when we wore out our welcome at the old folks' home. It's so tasty, even Pea Daddy likes it, when I wheel him over to the table, bend down a straw and coax a sip through his wrinkly lips.

Just making a smoothie for one? Scale the recipe down or pour extra smoothie into Popsicle molds and, trust me, someone will eat them.

INGREDIENTS

1½ tablespoons minced ginger

8–12 basil leaves

juice of 1 lime

2 cups non-dairy or organic milk

2 cups frozen blackberries

1 cup ice

organic sugar or stevia to taste

DIRECTIONS

1   Put ginger, basil, lime juice and milk in a blender and blend at high speed until ginger and basil are completely incorporated.

2   Add remaining ingredients and blend until smooth.

NUTRITION INFORMATION PER SERVING: 112 calories, 2 g total fat, 0 g saturated fat, 0 mg cholesterol, 61 mg sodium, 19 g carbohydrates, 4 g fiber, 5 g protein

chocolate almond cherry smoothie

Makes 4 smoothies

MY GRAMMY WOULD GIVE MY BROTHERS AND ME A BOX OF CHOCOLATE-covered cherries with our Christmas gifts each year. I'll chalk it up to a whim after seeing a big display at Walgreens, but after seeing our enthusiasm at being handed a box of candy that did not have my mom divvying out serving sizes, the whim became a tradition. Though my mom tried in vain to keep us from eating the whole box at once, I loved biting into the chocolates and getting the sweet surprise of a juicy, red treat too much to have just one. These smoothies channel those same chocolate and cherry flavors, but with a different surprise all together. Grammy never gave us spinach in those chocolates. Advantage Mama Pea.

INGREDIENTS

2 cups non-dairy or organic milk

3 tablespoons almond butter

1½ cups frozen cherries

1 banana

1 cup spinach

2 tablespoons cocoa powder

½ teaspoon almond extract

stevia to taste

1 cup ice cubes

DIRECTIONS

Combine all ingredients in a blender and blend until smooth. Pour and enjoy.

NUTRITION INFORMATION PER SERVING: 188 calories, 10 g total fat, 1 g saturated fat, 0 mg cholesterol, 74 mg sodium, 22 g carbohydrates, 4 g fiber, 7 g protein

mama pea's margarita smoothie

Makes 4 smoothies

I CONCOCTED THIS SMOOTHIE ON A RECENT CINCO DE MAYO, WHEN PEA
Daddy was working late, the girls had a little too much pep in their step and
I'd felt like I'd been blindfolded, spun around three times and beaten with a
stick. Though we enjoy the nonalcoholic version of these regularly for breakfast, there'll be no judgment here if you take matters into your own hands and
spice them up for your next fiesta. Olé!

INGREDIENTS

2 cups lime seltzer

1 cup light coconut milk

1 cup orange juice

½ cup lime juice

¼ cup chopped cilantro

2 cups spinach

2 cups frozen pineapple

1 cup ice

stevia to taste

sea salt to rim glasses

DIRECTIONS

1 Combine all ingredients except salt in a blender and blend until smooth.

2 Wet the rim of your serving glasses and dip in coarsely ground sea salt.
   Pour and enjoy.

NUTRITION INFORMATION PER SERVING: 195 calories, 12 g total fat, 11 g saturated fat,
0 mg cholesterol, 34 mg sodium, 23 g carbohydrates, 2 g fiber, 3 g protein

life's not fair blueberry scones

Makes 6 large scones

I HAD A RUDE AWAKENING AT THE STATE FAIR THIS summer. It seems it really isn't as fantastic of a place as I remember in my youth. Back then, just walking through the gates, getting an ink stamp on my hand that claimed that this year's fair was "The Big One," hearing the screams from the giant, flashing rides that towered above me and smelling the combination of curly fries, barn and Jacuzzi-salesperson cologne made me giddy.

My favorite ride was the Gravitron. It was a round, swirling hexagon of multicolored lights from the outside and a chamber of red pleather-covered sliding coffins inside, and I was convinced this must be what Space Camp is like, but it was only $6 a spin and Cletus Spuckler was behind the wheel instead of John Glenn. I'd ride it until I felt like I was still riding it when I got off, and then I'd ride it a few more times.

Much like nursing a hangover, I'd stumble to the scone booth and order some greasy, starchy, sugary goodness to make me feel "normal" again. The fair scone was a thing of beauty: a hot, flaky, melt-in-your-mouth berry-filled delight. I'd pass over cotton candy, elephant ears and corn dogs for just one fluffy biscuit of fair lovin'.

I couldn't wait to share the experience of the fair with Gigi and Lulu when we once again passed through the tacky gates and bore our stamps, claiming that perhaps the fair organizers were wrong and *this* year's fair was "The Big One." It didn't take long for me to realize that

breakfast at the IHOP

either the fair had changed, or I had. The rides looked like the same rides we had in 1986—literally, the *same exact rides.* That can't be safe. As Gigi excitedly ran to the Ferris wheel to see if she measured up, I kicked her shoes off and pressed down on her head to make sure she was a good four inches below the height requirement.

Having recently become a vegan, I was even more disappointed when we hit the barns to visit the animals. I managed to keep it together through the horses' stables, other than getting a little misty when I planted my Cole Haan directly in a pungent pile. But when we saw the dairy cows, with their swollen udders, solemn faces and mournful eyes, I lost it. I'd weaned Lulu just a few months before at the ripe old age of eighteen months, and after nursing her that long, I was just counting down the days until she showed less interest in my breasts than Pea Daddy. I set the bar very low. Yet standing there in the cement-floored barn with hundreds of strangers staring at the engorged animals, I realized that for these cows, that day of freedom would never come.

I immediately wanted, no, *needed,* a scone. After waiting in line for nearly twenty minutes, I plucked down my $6.50 and eagerly reached for the hot, paper-wrapped treat. Divided four ways, we each had just a taste. A taste was enough.

Pea Daddy turned to me and said, "These are a lot smaller than I remember." He had a similar reaction after Lulu was weaned.

"And, well, they just really aren't that great." Okay, now he was hurting my feelings.

But he was right, and I was inspired. I'm not saying that we won't shell out a pretty penny to take the girls to the fair each year. They looked at the sights and sounds with the same wide eyes and wonder that I did all those years ago. I'm just saying that we won't have the scones. We'll have my version. They've had a little work done, and they're spectacular.

INGREDIENTS

Scones:

½ cup non-dairy or organic milk

¼ cup vegan cream cheese (i.e., Tofutti Better Than Cream Cheese) or organic cream cheese

1 teaspoon lemon juice

½ teaspoon baking soda

2 cups whole wheat pastry or white whole wheat flour

½ cup organic sugar

1½ teaspoons baking powder

¼ teaspoon cream of tartar

½ teaspoon salt

½ cup vegan margarine (i.e., Earth Balance)

1 cup fresh blueberries

Glaze:

½ cup organic powdered sugar

1 tablespoon non-dairy or organic milk

¼ teaspoon almond extract (optional)

pea POINTS

These scones are quite large, so feel free to cut your rounds into smaller wedges for mini scones (you will likely need to reduce your baking time by a few minutes). Mini scones would be just great for a mini tea party, if you are into that kind of thing. We clearly are.

DIRECTIONS

1 Preheat oven to 350 degrees. Spray a baking sheet with cooking spray and set aside.

2 In a small bowl, blend the milk, cream cheese, lemon juice and baking soda, and set aside.

3 In a large bowl, mix the flour, sugar, baking powder, cream of tartar and salt. Cut in the margarine.

4 Stir the milk mixture into the flour mixture until just moistened. Mix in the blueberries.

5 Turn dough out onto a lightly floured surface, and knead briefly. Roll or pat dough into a 1-inch-thick round. Cut into 6 wedges, and place them 2 inches apart on the prepared baking sheet.

6 Bake 20 to 23 minutes, until golden brown on the bottom.

7 To prepare the glaze, whisk together powdered sugar, milk and almond extract, if using. Drizzle glaze over cooled scones.

NUTRITION INFORMATION PER SERVING: 273 calories, 4 g total fat, 1 g saturated fat, 5 mg cholesterol, 459 mg sodium, 56 g carbohydrates, 6 g fiber, 7 g protein

mini tofu frittatas

Makes 8 muffin-sized frittatas

GIGI HAS ALWAYS BEEN MY LITTLE UNINTENTIONAL VEGAN. THOUGH PEA Daddy and Lulu will do dairy, Gigi won't (knowingly) touch milk, cheese or eggs. Apparently ice cream is in a food group all by itself. Yet she enjoys these very quichelike mini frittatas despite their eggy appearance, texture and taste. I like to make these ahead of time and let Pea Daddy or Gigi grab one on the way out the door. They are full of vegetables and protein, and frankly, they just pack a lot better than ice cream.

INGREDIENTS

½ cup yellow onion, chopped (about ⅓ of a medium onion)

1 cup red pepper, chopped (about 1 medium pepper)

1 teaspoon minced garlic

salt and pepper, to taste

1 8-ounce can sliced olives, drained

1 cup organic spinach, chopped

¼ cup fresh basil, chopped

1 16-ounce package firm or extra firm tofu, drained and crumbled

¼ cup grated vegan or organic mozzarella cheese

1 tablespoon nutritional yeast

3 tablespoons soy sauce

pea POINTS

For a pizza-inspired take on these frittatas, add chopped veggie pepperoni slices and serve with a marinara dipping sauce.

DIRECTIONS

1 Preheat oven to 375 degrees. Spray 8 cups of a muffin tin with cooking spray.

2 Coat a large skillet with cooking spray and add chopped onion and red pepper. Sauté for 5 to 7 minutes until vegetables have softened. Add garlic and sauté for one additional minute. Season veggies with salt and pepper and add olives, spinach and basil. Set aside.

3 In a blender or food processor, add tofu, cheese, nutritional yeast and soy sauce. Blend or process until mixture is thick and creamy. Add tofu mixture to skillet with veggies and toss until fully integrated.

4 Scoop out ⅛ of mixture at a time and add to each cup of your prepared muffin tin.

5 Bake for 25 to 30 minutes or until top is slightly browned and firm to the touch.

NUTRITION INFORMATION PER SERVING: 134 calories, 9 g total fat, 1 g saturated fat, 1 mg cholesterol, 642 mg sodium, 6 g carbohydrates, 3 g fiber, 10 g protein

beg-worthy banana bread

Makes 1 loaf

POOR BANANA BREAD. IN A WORLD OF DELICIOUS BAKED GOODS, IT'S never at the top of anyone's list of favorites. I'm not sure it has to do with the bread itself, which, who are we kidding, should more accurately be called a cake, but more to do with the fact that no one ever plans to make banana bread. Banana bread is more of a tolerable accident, the incarnate of garbage and an attempt to rid your kitchen of fruit flies. Until now. After making this, you'll no longer be feeling sorry for banana bread, you'll have the whole family beggin' for it.

This bread is very moist, which means it goes fast. Literally. I keep my banana bread in the fridge to extend the shelf life.

INGREDIENTS

2 cups whole wheat pastry flour

1 teaspoon baking powder

½ teaspoon baking soda

¼ teaspoon salt

½ teaspoon cinnamon

½ teaspoon nutmeg

½ cup organic brown sugar

¼ cup vegan margarine (i.e., Earth Balance)

¼ cup almond butter

2 cups overripe bananas, mashed (about 3 bananas)

½ teaspoon almond extract

¼ cup non-dairy or organic milk

nuts and seeds, to sprinkle on top

DIRECTIONS

1   Preheat oven to 350 degrees.

2   In a large bowl, combine flour, baking powder, baking soda, salt, cinnamon and nutmeg.

3   In a medium-sized bowl, cream together brown sugar, margarine and almond butter, using a hand mixer or vigorously using a fork, and add mashed bananas. Add almond extract and milk and stir to combine.

4   Add wet ingredients to dry and stir until just combined.

5   Spread batter into a loaf pan sprayed with cooking spray, and scatter nuts and seeds on top.

6   Bake for 40 to 45 minutes, or until a toothpick inserted comes out clean. Let cool before slicing.

Variations:

Chocolate Chip Banana Bread: stir ⅔ cup high-quality chocolate chips into batter before baking.

Almond Flax Banana Bread: top batter with ⅓ cup chopped roasted almonds and 1 tablespoon flaxseeds before baking.

NUTRITION INFORMATION PER SERVING (for 12 slices): 170 calories, 5 g total fat, 1 g saturated fat, 0 mg cholesterol, 138 mg sodium, 30 g carbohydrates, 3 g fiber, 4 g protein

blueberry streusel muffins

Makes 12 muffins

MY KIDS FEEL LIKE THEY'RE GETTING AWAY WITH SOMETHING WHEN THEY get muffins for breakfast. The line between muffin and cupcake is indeed very thin. I'd reason that icing and perhaps sprinkles are the scandalous toppings that make a baked good in a paper cup a lady of the night, rather than a respectable breakfast. These muffins toe that line with their buttery, crumbly topping. Serve them for breakfast or even dessert, if you want. Just don't call them a cupcake.

INGREDIENTS

Muffins:

1½ cups whole wheat pastry flour

2 teaspoons baking powder

½ teaspoon baking soda

⅔ cup non-dairy milk or organic milk

1 teaspoon vanilla extract

⅓ cup orange juice

⅓ cup canola oil

½ cup organic sugar

1 cup fresh blueberries

Streusel Topping:

2 tablespoons brown sugar

1 tablespoon organic sugar

2 tablespoons whole wheat pastry or white whole wheat flour

2 tablespoons vegan margarine (i.e., Earth Balance)

3 tablespoons old-fashioned oats

1 teaspoon cinnamon

pea POINTS

If you want to use frozen blueber- ries, feel free to do so. Just don't mix them into the batter, but drop them in each indi- vidual muffin cup instead. Your bat- ter will turn gray otherwise. Gray may look good on Clooney, but not on muffins.

DIRECTIONS

1   Preheat oven to 400 degrees. Spray a muffin tin with cooking spray and set aside or line with muffin papers.

2   In a large bowl, combine flour, baking powder and baking soda and set aside.

3   In a smaller bowl, mix milk, vanilla, juice, oil and sugar.

4   Pour wet ingredients into dry ingredients and stir until just combined. Fold in blueberries.

5   In a small bowl, combine streusel ingredients with a fork until the topping is uniform and crumbly.

6   Spoon muffin batter into a prepared muffin tin, filling each cup ⅔ full. Top each cup with 1 to 2 teaspoons of streusel topping until it's all used up.

7   Bake for 20 to 23 minutes, or until a toothpick inserted comes out clean.

NUTRITION INFORMATION PER SERVING: 173 calories, 8 g total fat, 1 g saturated fat, 0 mg cholesterol, 24 mg sodium, 24 g carbohydrates, 3 g fiber, 3 g protein

breakfast at the IHOP

grand old biscuits

Makes 6 large biscuits

MY GRANNY WELCH MADE RENOWNED BISCUITS. THEY WERE ACTUALLY called "Granny Rolls," which also just so happened to be what she would call the pudgy baby skin that rolled over her baby great-grandchildren's legs. "Come over here and let me count those Granny Rolls!" she'd say as she lovingly pinched the little shar-pei folds. Her recipe was fairly basic, but definitely included some ingredients (namely, lard) that would put a few extra folds on you where they aren't quite as cute anymore. This is Granny's recipe with a Pea makeover. The secret to making them light and tender is Granny's technique of handling the dough as little as possible, while doubling over the dough to produce layer upon layer of flaky biscuit. The secret, my friends, is in the rolls.

For a quick dessert, use these biscuits as a shortcake with fresh organic berries. Sprinkle the top of the biscuits with a bit of organic sugar for a little extra special touch.

INGREDIENTS

¾ cup non-dairy or organic milk

1 teaspoon lemon juice

1 cup whole wheat pastry or white whole wheat flour

1 cup unbleached all-purpose flour

1 tablespoon baking powder

1 teaspoon salt

1 teaspoon organic sugar

¼ cup vegan margarine (i.e., Earth Balance)

DIRECTIONS

1 Preheat oven to 400 degrees. Spray a cookie sheet with cooking spray and set aside.

2 Combine milk and lemon juice and allow to "sour" by setting aside for approximately 5 minutes.

3 Sift dry ingredients into a large bowl. Cut in the margarine until the texture is like wet sand. Pour in soured milk and stir until just combined. Do not overmix.

4 Turn dough out onto a floured board and lightly roll into an approximately 11 × 9-inch rectangle. Add as much flour as necessary to keep dough from sticking, but be gentle.

5 Fold the dough in half, so it is "doubled over." Using a glass or a cookie cutter, cut dough into 6 rounds and transfer to the prepared cookie sheet.

6 Bake for 10 to 12 minutes.

NUTRITION INFORMATION PER SERVING: 174 calories, 3 g total fat, 1 g saturated fat, 0 mg cholesterol, 431 mg sodium, 32 g carbohydrates, 3 g fiber, 6 g protein

blackberry cinnamon rolls

Makes 8 rolls

I'VE ALWAYS LOVED A LAZY SUNDAY MORNING BREAKFAST. GROWING up, Sunday morning meant eggs and bacon, or sausage and pancakes; that is, until the day that my dad playfully threw a pancake at my mom, henceforth known as the infamous "Bisquick Cornea Assault of 1992."

I believe my mom was in the living room, feeling underappreciated for having made a special breakfast for our family when we ungratefully wanted cold cereal. I don't think you can blame us, though; we were almost at the end of the box of Cheerios, with a sexy box of Cocoa Krispies in the cupboard, just begging to be opened. Opening more than one box of cereal at a time was equivalent to opening my mom's pocketbook, pulling out a twenty and introducing it to a lighter. My dad tried to play the great appeaser by saying, "*You* can still have a pancake," and giving it a Frisbee-like toss at my mom. Bless her heart, she just wasn't ready for it and it caught her smack dab in her still sleep-encrusted eye.

If you ever meet my mom, please don't mention it. Trust me. According to her, "*You* don't understand, there was pancake *IN my eye*, and the dry mix was like glass *IN my eye*." Somehow, the incident gets brought up on every holiday and family gathering, and my mom's commitment to the severity of her injury hasn't wavered over the years. I'm frankly surprised she hasn't shown up with dark glasses, a Seeing Eye dog and a note from her optometrist diagnosing her with "irreparable vision impairment due to pancake in the eye." I am sure, as she reads this story, I will get a prompt phone call that starts with, "Sarah, *you* don't understand...."

Pancakes aside, for the most part I think Sunday mornings are about sitting around the table with bedhead, fighting over the comics and ads and taking the time to really sit down together and not rush off to school, work or that elusive 7:00 a.m. power sculpt class. I say "for the most part," because after making these cinnamon rolls, they have quickly become what Sunday mornings in our house are *all* about. I just wouldn't recommend throwing them.

peas and thank you

INGREDIENTS

Dough:

1 packet yeast

1 cup non-dairy or organic milk, briefly warmed to between 105 and 115 degrees

1½ cups whole wheat pastry or white whole wheat flour

1 cup organic unbleached all purpose flour, plus extra to roll dough

1 tablespoon baking powder

¼ cup organic sugar

½ teaspoon cinnamon

¼ teaspoon salt

¼ cup unsweetened applesauce

Cinnful Filling:

½ cup organic brown sugar

1 tablespoon cinnamon

2 tablespoons vegan margarine (i.e., Earth Balance), softened

1 pint of blackberries, washed and dried

Icing:

1 cup organic powdered sugar

¼ cup vegan cream cheese (i.e., Tofutti Better Than Cream Cheese) or organic cream cheese

few drops of vanilla extract

pinch of salt

DIRECTIONS

1 Dissolve yeast in warm milk. Set aside.

2 Combine whole wheat flour, all purpose flour, baking powder, sugar, cinnamon and salt.

3 In a separate bowl, combine filling ingredients minus the berries and set aside.

4 After yeast and milk mixture is foamy (about 5 to 8 minutes), stir in applesauce. Add applesauce mixture to dry dough ingredients and stir until a dough forms.

5 Turn dough out onto floured breadboard and knead for a minute or so (about 20 times). Knead in as much extra flour (approximately ¼ cup) as necessary, and keep kneading until dough is no longer sticky.

6 Roll dough into a large rectangle. Sprinkle filling over dough, and then scatter blackberries over the filling.

7 Roll dough up firmly to make a log. Cut the log into 8 equal pieces and place in an 8 × 8-inch pan sprayed with cooking spray.

8 Cover rolls with a clean towel and let rise in a warm place for at least 40 minutes before baking.

9 Preheat oven to 350 degrees. Bake rolls for 20 to 25 minutes.

10 Combine icing ingredients in a small bowl. Drizzle rolls with icing.

pea POINTS

My Peas wake up hungry, so I make the dough the night before and cover and place it in the refrigerator overnight. In the morning, I just let the dough rise for 40 minutes before baking.

For a more traditional roll, simply omit the blackberries, and add raisins and walnuts or pecans to the filling.

The Art of the Rise

Baking with yeast has always intimidated me. I've killed many a loaf by not nurturing the little life I brought into the world by opening an envelope and adding water. Here are a few tricks when working with yeast:

○ Get fresh with your yeast. Check the date on the package. Expired yeast can ruin your day and your rolls.

○ Hot water and milk can kill yeast. Use only lukewarm water or milk, ideally between 105 and 115 degrees.

○ Yeast cares about the environment. Dough should be left in a warm place, like a warm garage on a summer day or near a fireplace on a wintry afternoon. The ideal temperature is between 75 and 85 degrees.

○ Don't be too kneady. Knead to strengthen the gluten in the dough, but only until the surface of the dough is no longer sticky.

NUTRITION INFORMATION PER SERVING: 268 calories, 4 g total fat, 1 g saturated fat, 4 mg cholesterol, 147 mg sodium, 54 g carbohydrates, 4 g fiber, 6 g protein

apple cinnamon pancakes

Makes 10 large pancakes

ONE OF THE FIRST THINGS I EVER COOKED FOR PEA DADDY WAS A GREAT big stack of apple cinnamon pancakes. Uh…yes, future Gigi and Lulu, of course we, uh…had them one morning *after* we were married. Though the recipe I used then wasn't identical to this one (can you say "Bisquick"?), they did have the two key ingredients that make these pancakes so very satisfying: lots of cinnamon and even more apples. One taste of my apple cinnamon pancakes and Pea Daddy was hooked. Now that we have a family, we may not have, uh…apple cinnamon pancakes nearly as often, but they are even more unbelievable when we do.

pea
POINTS

Substitute blueberries for the apples or even chocolate chips for a special treat. Freeze any extras and heat in the toaster for the easiest pancake breakfast you'll ever make.

INGREDIENTS

1¾ cups whole wheat pastry or white whole wheat flour

¼ cup organic sugar

¼ teaspoon salt

1½ tablespoons baking powder

1 tablespoon ground cinnamon

1½ cups non-dairy or organic milk

1 large, organic apple, peeled and roughly chopped (about 1½ cups)

Toppings:
maple syrup and vegan margarine (i.e., Earth Balance)

DIRECTIONS

1 In a large bowl, whisk together flour, sugar, salt, baking powder and cinnamon.

2 Slowly add in milk, whisking just until batter is combined. Gently fold in chopped apples. Do not overmix.

3 Coat a large skillet or griddle with cooking spray and heat over medium heat. Scoop ⅓ cup batter into pan and cook 3 to 4 minutes until pancake edges start to brown and bubbles start to form. Flip and cook 2 to 3 minutes more.

4 Repeat with remaining batter. Serve with maple syrup and margarine.

NUTRITION INFORMATION PER SERVING (no toppings): 108 calories, 1 g total fat, 0 g saturated fat, 0 mg cholesterol, 78 mg sodium, 22 g carbohydrates, 3 g fiber, 4 g protein

self-serve oatmeal bar

Makes 4 adult-sized bowls of oats

IF YOU ASK GIGI AND LULU WHAT THEIR FAVORITE PART OF OUR RECENT vacation to Hawaii was, they aren't going to mention the luau. They certainly won't tell you about the burgers at Parker Cattle Ranch (have you been paying attention at all?). And though I'm sure they have fond memories of the sea turtles they were shooed away from for pestering, they won't even tell you about all the fun they had playing at the beach. No, Gigi and Lulu's mental postcard that they will carry around for the rest of their lives has less to do with palm trees and white sand and more to do with four little words: *self-serve frozen yogurt.*

I don't blame them, it was a virtual Willy Wonka scene when we walked in and saw ten whirring machines filled with flavors of air-filled, sugary, frozen dairy delights like peanut butter, mango, mint chocolate, peach, banana, cookies 'n' cream, cherry vanilla, banana foster, toasted coconut and Madagascar vanilla. Thank goodness Lulu was wearing a Pull-Ups because I think we all peed a little with excitement.

It didn't hurt at all that they gave us Kentucky Fried Chicken–sized tubs to haphazardly pump irresponsible amounts of fro yo into. If I had a dollar for every time I heard Lulu say, "I do it myself!" in that store, I'd have moved from our condo to the Ritz-Carlton.

The true euphoria hit, though, when we made our way to the toppings station. The girls took great pleasure in dumping on layer upon layer of M&M's, raspberries, Oreos, rainbow sprinkles, blueberries, chocolate chips, gummi bears and chocolate sauce until any sign of yogurt was gone. Pea Daddy gave himself a hernia as he lifted our vats of excess onto a scale, and then proceeded to have a heart attack as the cashier asked him for a mere $21.86.

Perhaps it was the relaxed state I was in, due to either the beauty of the tropics or the mango mojitos, but I suddenly had a moment of genius. Sure, overpriced junk-food-topped dairy is fine for vacation, but as the girls fished through their melting mounds of artificial colors and flavors to pick out the blueberries, I realized that I'd underutilized this self-serve mania on the mainland.

They weren't into the yogurt, they were into the sense of control, the independence, the right to bear ridiculously expensive, oversized desserts with obscene amounts of toppings, so help them God. Thus, the Self-Serve Oatmeal Bar was born. Goodbye fro yo, aloha breakfast!

INGREDIENTS

Oats:

2 cups old-fashioned oats

1 cup water

1 cup non-dairy or organic milk

pinch of salt

sweetener, if desired (i.e., organic brown sugar, stevia, agave, maple syrup or honey)

Optional Flavorings:

banana oats: 1 sliced banana

chocolate oats: 2 tablespoons cocoa powder

peanut butter oats: 2 tablespoons natural peanut butter

strawberry oats: ½ cup frozen or fresh berries

vanilla oats: 1 teaspoon vanilla extract

or any combination thereof

Topping Suggestions:

- roasted almonds, walnuts, pecans, pistachios or peanuts

- sliced bananas, strawberries, peaches or pineapple chunks

- fresh blueberries, blackberries or raspberries

- almond butter, peanut butter or sunflower butter

- ground flaxseed, toasted coconut, pepitas or sunflower seeds

- crumbled Blueberry Streusel Muffins (p. 20), Anytime Cookies (p. 200), Almond Joy Cookie Bars (p. 211), or Life's Not Fair Blueberry Scones (p. 13)

- brown sugar, maple syrup or agave

pea POINTS

Oats are my favorite way to start the day. The fiber and protein found in this whole grain are truly satiating and keep away those pre-lunch grumbles. I mix a little brown rice protein powder in mine for an extra protein punch.

DIRECTIONS

1 Combine oats, water, milk and salt in a large pot and bring to a boil. Reduce heat and add in any base flavorings you would like. Lower heat and continue to simmer oats for five minutes, stirring frequently until they are thick and creamy.

2 Prepare toppings by putting small amounts of each in mini serving dishes with small spoons and placing them on a Lazy Susan or in the center of the table.

3 Place oats in serving bowls and allow your family to top their own bowls to their little hearts' desires.

NUTRITION INFORMATION PER SERVING (no toppings): 178 calories, 4 g total fat, 1 g saturated fat, 0 mg cholesterol, 32 mg sodium, 30 g carbohydrates, 4 g fiber, 7 g protein

fabulous french toast

Makes 4 to 6 slices

I AM A HESITANT FRENCH TOAST FAN. I COULD ALWAYS TELL WHEN MY mom was making it by the crinkle of bread wrappers and the smell of vanilla and cinnamon coming from the kitchen. Even as a kid, I didn't like eggs, so while I loved the warm maple syrup drowning the slightly sweet and doughy bread, I always hated when I'd get an eggy edge of crust. In my book, eggs and syrup are a combination more distasteful than Katie Holmes and Tom Cruise. Something's not right. With this fabulous and egg-free recipe, though, problem solved.

INGREDIENTS

4 to 6 slices bread

⅓ cup non-dairy or organic milk

⅓ cup non-dairy or organic creamer

2 tablespoons whole wheat pastry or white whole wheat flour

1 tablespoon nutritional yeast

½ teaspoon cinnamon

1 teaspoon vanilla extract

Optional Toppings:
vegan margarine (i.e., Earth Balance), maple syrup, fresh sliced berries or bananas, powdered sugar or any combination thereof

pea POINTS

Don't be afraid of the nutritional yeast in this recipe. Not only is it a great vegan source of vitamin B_{12}, but it gives the French toast a slightly nutty flavor. It's truly delicious!

DIRECTIONS

1   Combine all ingredients except bread in a shallow dish. Whisk well to get rid of any lumps.

2   Dip bread on each side and carefully place in a preheated skillet sprayed with cooking spray, cooking for several minutes on each side. Serve with optional toppings.

NUTRITION INFORMATION PER SERVING (for 6 slices): 99 calories, 2 g total fat, 0 g saturated fat, 0 mg cholesterol, 145 mg sodium, 16 g carbohydrates, 2 g fiber, 4 g protein

breakfast at the IHOP

whole wheat ginger pear waffles

Makes approximately 6 waffles

WHEN LULU WAS BORN AND WE TOOK ON THE DAUNTING CHALLENGE of having two kids under the age of three, we fell into some routines pretty quickly. I would nurse Lulu every two hours between 9:00 p.m. and 6:00 a.m., and then after that last half hour of propping myself up in a stiff armchair,

pleading with the sun to not come up, I'd sleep in as long as humanly possible until the feeding frenzy would start again. It's no wonder I own stock in Wonderbra—"the girls" have been through a lot. Lulu had no interest in a bottle (a trend I hope will carry her through college and beyond) so Pea Daddy was fairly helpless when it came to providing any relief in the nightly milkfest.

His role, in theory, was to get Gigi up each morning, quietly tiptoe past a sleeping Mommy and Lulu, float down the stairs as if on air, and get breakfast in such a peaceful manner that I'd begin to think I had hearing loss from Lulu's middle-of-the-night crying.

In theory.

In reality, Gigi, though perfectly capable of getting out of her toddler bed on her own, would begin shouting, "Dad-dy! Dad-dy! Dad-dy!" with such a precise and consistent tone that it could have easily been mistaken for the neighbor's car alarm. Pea Daddy would throw back the covers in disgust and sigh heavily while I nestled deeper in the sheets and smiled a not-the-least-bit empathetic smile. The smile faded quickly as Gigi would open and slam each of her dresser drawers with vigor and determination, searching for just the right breakfast-eating attire, even though a blind monkey could tell you that all of her tutus were in the top drawer. "I found it!" she'd holler, stuffing all of her once neatly folded clothes back into the drawer and then again slamming it shut.

"Shhh...." You had to give Pea Daddy credit for trying. Gigi would flounce down the hall, less like a pirouetting prima ballerina and more like a drunk hippo in Doc Martens. With each step downstairs, Gigi announced a hearty, "Step Number One! Step Number Two! Step Number Three! Step Number Four..." memorializing the journey. We have exactly sixteen steps, though we'd always end up with "Step Number Eleventeen!" or "Step Number Twelveteen!" Blame who you will, but I'm choosing that smarmy "Joe" from *Blue's Clues*.

Once the two had made their ear-splitting mecca to the kitchen, I could overhear a brief discussion about what breakfast would be. Pea Daddy, bless his heart, was limited in both time and skill as to what he could prepare.

"Peanut butter oatmeal!" Gigi said with enthusiasm.

"Again?" Pea Daddy groaned. "How about a bagel?"

"Peanut butter oatmeal!" Gigi chimed louder.

"Cereal?" Pea Daddy offered.

"Peanut butter oatmeal! Peanut butter oatmeal! Peanut butter oatmeal!"

Gigi wasn't giving in. Pea Daddy had eaten peanut butter oatmeal every morning for breakfast for the last five months. I'd caught him trying to stack the deck against Gigi by emptying the oats container into the trash and furiously eating peanut butter out of the jar as if the high school quarterback had broken up with him the night before.

As the wailing started, and Pea Daddy tried to find a way to convince Gigi that a bowl of cold cereal was just as delicious as creamy, nutty oats, I knew I had to help. My ability to form coherent thoughts later depended on it. Oh, I wasn't getting up to whip up some pancakes or a batch of scones. I wasn't dragging my sore nipples out of bed to cook even if the president, Oprah and Ryan Reynolds were waiting in the breakfast nook.

However, Sunday waffles easily turn into weekday toaster waffles when you make a double batch and freeze the extra. I'm making no promises that your kids won't love these so much that they will want them every morning for the next five months. Tutus are optional.

INGREDIENTS

1½ cups whole wheat pastry or white whole wheat flour

¾ teaspoon ground cinnamon

1½ teaspoons ground ginger

½ teaspoon ground nutmeg

1 tablespoon organic sugar

2 teaspoons baking powder

½ teaspoon salt

½ cup sparkling water

½ cup non-dairy or organic milk

2 tablespoons canola oil

½ teaspoon vanilla extract

1 pear, peeled and chopped (approximately 1 cup)

Toppings:
vegan margarine (i.e., Earth Balance) and maple syrup

DIRECTIONS

1   Preheat waffle iron, first spraying with a cooking spray.

2   Combine flour, spices, sugar, baking powder and salt in a large bowl.

3   In a smaller bowl, combine sparkling water, milk, oil and vanilla.

4   Pour the wet ingredients into the dry, and stir until just combined. Gently fold in chopped pear. Do *not* overmix.

5   Spoon about ⅓ cup of batter into each waffle well and close iron. Cook waffles for several minutes, until waffles are golden brown.

6   Serve with margarine and maple syrup.

NUTRITION INFORMATION PER SERVING (no toppings): 174 calories, 6 g total fat, 1 g saturated fat, 0 mg cholesterol, 206 mg sodium, 28 g carbohydrates, 5 g fiber, 5 g protein

pea POINTS

Freeze these waffles in resealable plastic bags and then just pop them in the toaster like you would store-bought toaster waffles. These waffles are higher in fiber, lower in sugar and preservative free, not to mention far cheaper. Go ahead, L'Eggo of those other ones.

peas and thank you

baked oatmeal squares

Makes 9 2 × 3-inch squares

THERE'S NOTHING I LOVE MORE THAN A BREAKFAST THAT I CAN PREPARE the night before, except maybe a breakfast that someone else can prepare the night before. I'm a dreamer. Still, I love throwing this oatmeal together on a Saturday night and then buying myself a few extra minutes on Sunday morning to sip my coffee, change any sheets due to overzealous Saturday night juice drinking and explain why a swimsuit, hula skirt and lei are not acceptable Sunday School wear. Where were those waterproof suits after last night's juice-swigging fest? Perhaps that's another detail I could have worked out the night before.

INGREDIENTS

2 cups old-fashioned oats

¼ cup to ½ cup organic brown sugar (depending on how sweet you like your oatmeal)

2 teaspoons ground cinnamon

2 teaspoons baking powder

1 teaspoon salt

½ cup dried cranberries

1 cup non-dairy or organic milk

½ block silken tofu

½ cup applesauce

1 teaspoon vanilla extract

Toppings:
non-dairy milk, sliced bananas, berries, nut butter, et cetera

DIRECTIONS

1 Preheat oven to 350 degrees or mixture can be made ahead of time and refrigerated overnight, to be baked in the morning.

2 In a large bowl, combine oats, sugar, cinnamon, baking powder, salt and cranberries.

3 In a blender or food processor, combine wet ingredients and process until smooth. Add wet ingredients to dry and mix well.

4 Spread mixture into an 8 × 8-inch pan that has been sprayed with cooking spray and either bake immediately or refrigerate. If baking immediately, bake for approximately 40 minutes. If baking the next day, the oats will have absorbed some of the moisture and will need to bake for only approximately 30 minutes.

5 Cut into squares and pass desired toppings at the table.

NUTRITION INFORMATION PER SERVING: 143 calories, 2 g total fat, 0 g saturated fat, 0 mg cholesterol, 277 mg sodium, 26 g carbohydrates, 2 g fiber, 5 g protein

pumpkin cream pie oat bran

Makes 4 large bowls

I USED TO LOVE HOT CEREAL WHEN I WAS A KID, SAVE FOR ONE LITTLE thing: the lumps. There'd be nothing better than working my way through a hot, creamy bowl, flooded with a pat of butter; that is, until my spoon would hit a grainy nugget of starchy, chewy cereal. Somehow this never happened to the rosy-cheeked little boy on the commercials, who, just in from playing in the snow and hunched over a steamy bowl, never spat a mouthful out in disgust and shouted, "What are you trying to do, woman, kill me?!" Sorry, Mom. This delicious breakfast is reminiscent of cold fall mornings. It is topped with a pat of satisfying, melting nut butter and its preparation technique ensures that there's nary a lump.

pea POINTS

Even without blending, this oat bran is creamy and delicious. Substitute banana slices for the canned pumpkin and they will virtually melt into the oat bran.

INGREDIENTS

1 cup canned pumpkin

1 cup water

1½ cups non-dairy or organic milk, divided

1½ teaspoons ground cinnamon

½ teaspoon freshly grated nutmeg

pinch of salt

sweetener (i.e., organic sugar, organic brown sugar, stevia, maple syrup or agave to taste)

1⅓ cups oat bran

¼ cup almond butter

DIRECTIONS

1 Combine pumpkin, water, 1 cup of milk, cinnamon, nutmeg, salt and sweetener in a medium pot. Cover and bring to a boil over medium heat.

2 Stir in oat bran and cook for 2 minutes.

3 Carefully pour contents of pot into a high-speed blender. Add remaining milk, 2 tablespoons at a time, and blend at high speed until mixture is creamy and smooth.

4 Return mixture to pot and reheat until thoroughly warmed. Serve each bowl with a tablespoon of almond butter on top.

NUTRITION INFORMATION PER SERVING: 234 calories, 13 g total fat, 2 g saturated fat, 0 mg cholesterol, 51 mg sodium, 32 g carbohydrates, 8 g fiber, 11 g protein

breakfast at the IHOP

tofu scrambles

Makes 4 servings

WE ARE ALWAYS LATE FOR CHURCH.

Our church offers three services: 8:15, 9:45 and 11:15 a.m. You can bet we are always at the 11:15 service…at exactly 11:30. I could blame it on the fact that we refuse to set an alarm on the weekend, but the truth is, we haven't set an alarm for five years. You do the math.

I'm having a hard time recalling at exactly what age I stopped wanting to get up at 4:30 a.m. to watch cartoons. I'd creep into my parents' room in my pink Winnie the Pooh footies from which, unfortunately, the little piggie who "went to market" was trying to lodge his escape. I'd get no more than three centimeters from my peacefully sleeping mother's face, wait exactly eight seconds to see if she was breathing and then shout, "Are 'tartoons on yet, Mom?!" Once my father grabbed the paddles and shocked my mother's heart back into rhythm, she'd point out that it was still dark outside and that the only thing on TV were test patterns. Of course, I already knew this because I'd taught myself how to turn on the TV about six months earlier and had been awake for an hour already, staring at "the rainbow" and trying to pick out my favorite color.

The insomniac doesn't fall far from the tree, and now it's Gigi who is waking at inappropriate hours. Fortunately, Pea Daddy's side of the bed is closer to our bedroom door, and the girls have been appropriately conditioned to wake Daddy, and Daddy alone. Chocolate-covered raisins aren't just for potty training, my friends.

Our tardiness for church lies not in oversleeping, but in the need to try to cram as many things in before church as possible. Chocolate-covered raisins also apply here.

Lawn maintenance? Check.

His and Her Workouts? Check.

Laundry? Check.

Ballet recital/fashion show/tea parties/pedicures? Quadruple check.

Even on days when we are out of the house at 10:45 a.m., there's always

peas and thank you

something that makes us late, such as an argument about which of the three car seat buckles Lulu is going to fasten by herself. The answer is three.

So when we roll into church at 11:30 a.m. each week, our usual pew is waiting for us, our pew neighbors have programs ready to hand us and the pastor, mid-prayer, throws in a statement about "being diligent in the Lord," as his eyebrow raises in our direction. We would surely be forgiven if we sat quietly, sang on key or did not shriek, "I WANT GUM!!!" while pushing a gigantic purse that sounds as if it is filled with metal chains, maracas and janitor's keys off the pew bench when it cascades to the floor. Then there are the eleven trips from our pew to the bathroom, the library, the Children's Message, the nursery and back again to retrieve a clean diaper and the entire contents of the wipes container thanks to the lovely "offering" that Lulu has made to the child care workers.

Actual time spent at church today: 1 hour and 13 minutes.

Actual time spent in prayer, meditation or connecting to God: 47 seconds.

The more quick-and-easy options for breakfast we have, the better. With this tofu dish, which is almost indistinguishable from scrambled eggs, our plates are clean in a hurry.

I'll try to remember to thank God if we make it on time next Sunday.

INGREDIENTS

1 16-ounce block organic firm tofu
(drained, crumbled and squeezed dry)

1 teaspoon minced garlic

½ teaspoon cumin

½ teaspoon turmeric

1 teaspoon lemon juice

1 tablespoon reduced sodium soy
sauce or tamari

1 tablespoon nutritional yeast

⅓ cup sliced mushrooms

⅓ cup diced red pepper
(about ½ a medium pepper)

⅓ cup diced tomato

2 teaspoons diced onion

DIRECTIONS

1 Drain, crumble, squeeze and pat dry tofu. Add all seasonings. Stir until
evenly coated and set aside for at least ten minutes for flavors to absorb.

2 Spray a large skillet with cooking spray and place over medium-high heat.
Add vegetables and sauté until they are tender. Add tofu and cook until
warmed through and golden, about five minutes.

NUTRITION INFORMATION PER SERVING: 130 calories, 7 g total fat, 1 g saturated fat,
0 mg cholesterol, 146 mg sodium, 6 g carbohydrates, 2 g fiber, 13 g protein

pea POINTS

Tofu is high in protein, but without the saturated fat and cholesterol of eggs. Scrambles make a great breakfast-for-dinner option or try them Pea Daddy's favorite way: wrapped up in a tortilla with salsa for a makeshift breakfast burrito.

Beyond Pea B and J: Lunches, Salads and Soups

I LOVE LUNCH.

When the girls were babies, I would eagerly await the sound of Pea Daddy's car pulling in the garage almost every day as he came home to eat lunch and see his girls. Unfortunately, at least one of us smelled like dirty diapers and spit-up, and it was almost always me. I'd hand over the girls and make a run for the quickest yet most enjoyable shower of my life, slap on a fresh coat of mascara and deodorant, prioritized in just that order, take a swig of mouthwash and then tear down the stairs to put together something for Pea Daddy to eat before he'd have to turn right around and make the twenty-minute drive to work. I was grateful for his sacrifice, and at least if I could give him a healthy meal before sending him back to the office, I felt slightly less guilty about it.

Now that the girls are older, Pea Daddy doesn't come home for lunch as often. Though now I smell of Play-Doh and craft glue, on most days by lunchtime I've managed to accomplish a certain degree of hygiene on my own, albeit with a scrutinizing audience. "You should wear this dress, Mommy!" insists Gigi, pulling the black lace strapless number I wore to our rehearsal dinner. I had no idea lunch was so formal. The fact of the matter is, it isn't. We munch on salads, sandwiches and smoothies most days, and I pack something for Pea Daddy to take to the office.

The recipes in this section are all delicious, whether for a light dinner for all of us, a midday feast for the girls and me, or something to tuck in Pea Daddy's briefcase. I know that day will come for the girls, when I'll pack embarrassing notes on napkins and non-traditional sandwich creations in My Little Pony lunch boxes. For now, though, I look forward to the time each day that I have them to myself, to have our leisurely lunches, no matter how overdressed I may be.

crack wrap

Makes 4 wraps

I'D BE LYING IF I SAID THAT BEING A NEW MOM WAS ALWAYS A JOY.
Truth be told, one of my greatest joys of my daughters' early childhoods were the magical two hours of each day called "Nap Time."

Oooh, that's good. Say it again.

Nap time.

Mmm.

All of my mommy friends gave me the advice early on about how to manage the sleep deprivation of new motherhood. "Sleep when they sleep!" I was told time and time again. Pardon me?! You want me to take the only two hours I have in a twenty-four-hour period when I can pee without guilt, or a witness, and sleep? I think not. My daily routine centered around nap time like I had a court date with a threatened prison term if I didn't show up.

Some typical exchanges:

Friend: Can you come for a cup of tea?

Me: If you drink fast and talk faster.

Friend: Can you give me a ride to the mechanic this afternoon?

Me: I hear walking is great exercise.

Friend: I think you need medical attention for the dislocated shoulder you
suffered lowering the sleeping baby into her crib without waking her.

Me: Pass the Ben-Gay, I'm not leaving until 4:00 o'clock.

Once I finally did get the little angels down, their white noise machines humming loudly enough to drown out my hoots and squeals of delight as I made my way down the hall, I would be beside myself with how to spend the next blissful 118 minutes. Shaking with excitement and hunger, I'd make my way to the kitchen. I needed sustenance. I needed comfort. I needed warm melty goodness in a toasty tortilla. Yoga can wait. The *Real Housewives* aren't going anywhere. Why shower when I haven't left the house for three days and you "don't want my stinkin' ride to the mechanic anyway!"?

This recipe was created with one person and only one person in mind. Me. Ragged-yoga-pants-with-the-exhausted-waistband-wearing, weepy-eyed and

leaky-breasted me. This grown-up grilled cheese was chicken soup for this mommy's soul, and it was mine, all mine!

At least it *was*. Nap time is a thing of the past now, as is sole ownership of the deliciousness that is the Crack Wrap. Eat up, girls. Mommy's going to take a nap.

INGREDIENTS

4 La Hacienda de Peas Tortillas (p. 102) or store-bought whole wheat variety

1 cup Crazy Good Hummus (p. 116) or store-bought variety

1 to 2 ounces shredded or sliced non-dairy Swiss or mozzarella cheese (i.e., Daiya mozzarella shreds) or organic Swiss or mozzarella cheese

1 to 2 teaspoons melted vegan margarine (i.e., Earth Balance) or cooking spray

DIRECTIONS

1 Place a medium skillet over medium-high heat.

2 Spread your tortilla or wrap with a generous amount of hummus and top with cheese. Tuck both ends of the tortilla up and roll like a burrito.

3 Brush the outside of the wrap with a light coating of melted margarine or a quick blast of cooking spray. Grill wrap on both sides until the outside is toasted and the cheese has melted.

NUTRITION INFORMATION PER SERVING: 276 calories, 10 g total fat, 1 g saturated fat, 0 mg cholesterol, 452 mg sodium, 39 g carbohydrates, 4 g fiber, 8 g protein

pea POINTS

Served with a soul-soothing soup, e.g., Cashew Carrot Ginger Soup (p. 67) or Spicy African Peanut Slow Cooker Soup (p. 75), this makes the ultimate comfort food on those days when we all need a little extra comfort.

beyond Pea B and J

picnic tortilla pinwheels

Makes 12 mini pinwheels

Our life is spent on the living room floor.

I've slept in a tent on the living room floor.

We dance to some tunes on the living room floor.

Find unexplained spoons on the living room floor.

Sometimes we read on the living room floor.

Somebody peed on the living room floor.

So much we've achieved on the living room floor,
Perhaps was conceived on the living room floor.

We laid a sheet on the living room floor.
So we could eat on the living room floor!

For all the good times on the living room floor,
And silly rhymes on the living room floor,

When they're grown and gone from the living room floor,
I'll remember fondly good times on the living room floor.

INGREDIENTS

6 slices tempeh bacon
(i.e., Lightlife Fakin' Bacon)

4 La Hacienda de Peas Tortillas
(p. 102) or store-bought whole
wheat variety

⅓ cup non-dairy (i.e., Tofutti Better Than
Cream Cheese) or organic cream cheese

1 thinly sliced organic apple, any variety

1 cup fresh organic spinach leaves

DIRECTIONS

1   Cook bacon according to package directions.

2   Lay out tortillas and spread each with 1 to 2 tablespoons of cream cheese.
    Layer 1½ bacon slices, apple and spinach in each tortilla and roll tightly.

3   Cut into thirds and serve, securing with toothpicks, if necessary.

NUTRITION INFORMATION PER SERVING: 115 calories, 6 g total fat, 1 g saturated fat,
4 mg cholesterol, 330 mg sodium, 12 g carbohydrates, 1 g fiber, 4 g protein

untraditional broccoli salad

Makes 6 to 8 servings

IF YOU ARE WITH ME THUS FAR, YOU LIKELY HAVE ONE burning question: "For Pete's sake, how do I potluck?!" Forget the Swedish meatballs. Don't even think about the deviled eggs. The pistachio salad with cottage cheese and marshmallows is definitely out. (That dish always rubbed me the wrong way anyway. Cottage cheese, pistachios, whipped topping and pineapple have no business being in the same bowl.)

But what about broccoli salad? Everyone loves that creamy, crunchy salad studded with bacon bits, cranberries, red onion and sunflower seeds, and if it gets the crowd to eat broccoli, it's almost worth overlooking the bacon and mayo. Almost. This version may be untraditional, but that just means it's better. I'll get cracking on making over that pistachio salad. It has nowhere to go but up.

INGREDIENTS

1 package tempeh bacon (i.e., Lightlife Fakin' Bacon)

5 cups broccoli florets

½ cup dried cherries, chopped

¼ cup red onion, minced (optional)

2 tablespoons organic sugar or stevia

3 tablespoons red wine vinegar

1 cup reduced-fat vegan mayonnaise (i.e., Reduced Fat Vegenaise)

1 cup cashews, coarsely chopped

DIRECTIONS

1 Place bacon in a large, deep skillet that has been coated with cooking spray. Cook over medium-high heat until evenly brown. Crumble and set aside.

2 In a large bowl, toss together broccoli, dried cherries and red onions, if using.

3 In a separate bowl, whisk together the sugar or stevia, vinegar and mayonnaise. Pour over broccoli mixture and toss to coat. Refrigerate for at least 2 hours.

4 Before serving, sprinkle with cashews and crumbled bacon. Toss and serve.

NUTRITION INFORMATION PER SERVING (for 8 servings): 232 calories, 18 g total fat, 2 g saturated fat, 0 mg cholesterol, 363 mg sodium, 13 g carbohydrates, 6 g fiber, 7 g protein

The longer you refrigerate this salad, the more tender the broccoli will get, making it a bit easier for tiny Peas to chew. Because the dressing is dairy-free, you won't need to worry about leaving this salad out a bit longer than the mayonnaise-based original.

57

beyond Pea B and J

chickpea strawberry mango salad

Makes 4 entrée-sized salads

GIGI AND LULU NEVER MET A FRUIT THEY DIDN'T LIKE. IN FACT, AT LUNCH and dinner we generally have to hold back their fruit bowl until they've eaten a good portion of their entrée, or else breakfast, lunch and dinner would look like a VH1 reality show: totally fruity. Yet when we serve up this salad for dinner on a summer night, our girls get to have their fruit and eat it too.

INGREDIENTS

8 cups romaine lettuce, washed, dried and torn into bite-sized pieces

1 batch Pumpkin Spice–Roasted Chickpeas (p. 105) or 1 14-ounce can chickpeas, drained and rinsed

1 mango, peeled and cut into chunks

2 cups strawberries, washed and sliced

½ cup dried cranberries

½ cup roasted almonds, roughly chopped

¼ cup fresh mint, chopped

1 batch Cinnamon Vinaigrette (p. 126)

pea POINTS

For an even "meatier" version, add meatless chicken strips, nuggets or patties, cut into bite-sized chunks. To make it a meal, serve with Cowgirl Cornbread (p. 101), Soft Pretzel Twists (p. 98) or some whole-grain bread.

DIRECTIONS

Place lettuce in individual serving dishes and top with ¼ of the chickpeas, mango chunks, strawberry slices, cranberries, almonds and mint. Dress with Cinnamon Vinaigrette.

NUTRITION INFORMATION PER SERVING: 254 calories, 7 g total fat, 1 g saturated fat, 0 mg cholesterol, 189 mg sodium, 45 g carbohydrates, 9 g fiber, 7 g protein

beyond Pea B and J

lemon lentil soup

Makes 6 large bowls

I'M GRATEFUL I DON'T HAVE A GREEK GRANDMOTHER, BECAUSE IF I DID, she'd likely disown me for messing with the classic Greek soup, *Avgolemono*. The original Greek recipe is rich, lemony and satisfying, but so is this version, with fresh lemons, cashew cream and hearty red lentils. You might just think you are at a Greek café overlooking white sandy beaches, topaz waters and John Stamos. Even grandma has to admit that sounds tasty.

INGREDIENTS

4 carrots, peeled and chopped (about 2 cups)

2 stalks celery, chopped (about 1 cup)

¾ teaspoon coriander

4 cups organic vegetable broth

1 cup red lentils, rinsed and drained

¼ cup fresh lemon juice

3 tablespoons raw cashews

1½ cups chopped spinach

2 tablespoons chopped parsley

salt and pepper to taste

DIRECTIONS

1   In a saucepan over medium-high heat and sprayed with cooking spray, sauté carrots, celery and coriander for approximately 5 minutes or until vegetables are tender.

2   Add broth and red lentils and bring to a boil. Reduce heat, cover and simmer for 15 minutes, until lentils are tender but not mushy.

3   Combine lemon juice and cashews in a food processor or blender. When lentils are done, stir in spinach, parsley and lemon-cashew cream and heat until mixture is uniform.

4   Adjust salt and pepper to taste.

NUTRITION INFORMATION PER SERVING: 170 calories, 3 g total fat, 0 g saturated fat, 0 mg cholesterol, 421 mg sodium, 28 g carbohydrates, 12 g fiber, 10 g protein

beyond Pea B and J

un-toppable black bean soup (page 64)

un-toppable black bean soup

Makes 6 to 8 servings

YOU CAN FIND BLACK BEAN SOUP ON MANY A RESTAURANT MENU THESE days, but in my not-so-humble opinion, it doesn't hold a candle to this one. Packed with vegetables, beans and spices, this soup is a perfect blend of tex-

tures. Even better, it just begs to play dress up like Gigi and Lulu, but instead of tiaras and tutus, this is perfect with non-dairy or organic sour cream and cheese, freshly chopped cilantro and tortilla strips. At home, you get to control the quality of the ingredients, how chunky or smooth you want the soup and best of all, you get to play dress up as much as you want. Around here, that's never a problem.

INGREDIENTS

1½ cups chopped onion

2 cups carrots, peeled and sliced

2 teaspoons minced garlic

1 tablespoon ground cumin

1 teaspoon dried oregano

1 teaspoon dried basil

½ teaspoon chili powder

2 19-ounce cans black beans, rinsed and drained

5 cups vegetable stock

1 cup low-sodium V8 vegetable juice, or use your own tomato vegetable juice blend

salt and pepper to taste

Garnishes:
chopped fresh cilantro, non-dairy or organic sour cream and cheese, tortilla strips or chips, olives, chopped tomatoes

DIRECTIONS

1 Spray a large stockpot with cooking spray and heat over medium-high heat. Add onion and cook until starting to soften, approximately 4 minutes.

2 Add carrots, garlic, cumin, oregano, basil and chili powder and sauté for an additional 4 minutes.

3 Add beans, stock and vegetable juice and bring to a boil. Reduce heat and simmer for 20 minutes.

4 Allow soup to cool slightly then remove half and place it in a high-speed blender, pureeing until smooth. Return smooth soup back to the pot and repeat process, if necessary, to reach desired consistency. Alternatively, you can use an immersion blender directly in the pot to reach desired consistency.

5 Adjust salt and pepper to taste and then serve. Pass garnishes at the table.

NUTRITION INFORMATION PER SERVING (for 8 servings): 142 calories, 0 g total fat, 0 g saturated fat, 0 mg cholesterol, 877 mg sodium, 27 g carbohydrates, 9 g fiber, 8 g protein

pea POINTS

Freeze leftovers of this soup and defrost for a quick weeknight dinner. Serve with quesadillas made with La Hacienda de Peas Tortillas (p. 102) and non-dairy or organic cheese, and green salad.

beyond Pea B and J

cashew carrot ginger soup

Makes 4 large bowls

ONE OF THE FIRST CONCERNS MY MOM HAD WHEN she heard we were going vegetarian was how we would ever replace chicken noodle soup. With two kids who attract germs like magnets ("Quit licking the shopping cart, Lulu!"), it was a valid concern. I have to admit, at first I was a bit confused myself at what to feed a cold with. But comfort isn't always found where you expect it, as evidenced by the mangy shred of polyester Lulu totes around known as "Blankie."

This is no chicken soup like Mama made, but it is warm, creamy, a little spicy and totally soothing. Sleep a little easier, Mimi Pea. I've got it covered.

pea POINTS

You can substitute sweet potatoes or butternut squash for the carrots, if you'd like. Just peel, cube and adjust your steaming time accordingly. Garam masala is an Indian spice blend that you can find at most major supermarkets. If you can't find it, feel free to use extra curry powder in its place.

INGREDIENTS

6 to 8 carrots, peeled and chopped (about 3 cups)

1 cup light coconut milk

¼ cup raw cashews

2 cups organic vegetable stock

3 tablespoons chopped ginger

2 teaspoons minced garlic

1 tablespoon curry powder

1 teaspoon garam masala

½ teaspoon coriander

½ teaspoon cinnamon

organic sugar or stevia to taste

½ teaspoon salt

additional salt and pepper to taste

DIRECTIONS

1   Steam carrots until tender.

2   Combine carrots and remaining ingredients in a blender and puree until smooth.

3   Transfer soup to a saucepan and heat through. Adjust seasonings to taste.

NUTRITION INFORMATION PER SERVING: 206 calories, 15 g total fat, 9 g saturated fat, 0 mg cholesterol, 639 mg sodium, 16 g carbohydrates, 5 g fiber, 4 g protein

tempeh bacon reubens

Makes 4 sandwiches

THE DAY I FOUND OUT WHAT GOES INTO A REUBEN SANDWICH WAS MUCH like the day I found out about how babies are made. As soon as the conversation started, I wanted out. I was a little embarrassed, somewhat nauseated and completely disappointed.

Ever since I was old enough to care about clothes, my mom and I have had a birthday tradition of going shopping and out to lunch. We didn't have a lot of extra money as a one-income family, and since I had two brothers and was five-foot-eleven with a mom who was five-foot-two, I often wound up wearing my grandmother's hand-me-downs. Lucky for me, she had great taste, yet I can't help but think that a pair of Liz Claiborne blue moccasin loafers looked out of place on a seventh-grader. I know of at least one burly eighth-grade girl with a mustache who agreed and wasn't afraid to let me know it. Daily.

So every year, it really was a special treat to get to go to Portland to pick out a new outfit that wasn't designed for a sixty-two-year-old retiree and to choose wherever I wanted to eat lunch. On the year that my world forever changed, we were in the food court of the mall, my hand clenched tight around a shopping bag of fuchsia stirrup pants and a drop-waist dress with a floral pattern reminiscent of my great-grandma's polyester couch. My mom spotted Rose's Deli, a famed Portland restaurant known for its classic Reuben sandwiches.

"Oh, we have to go get a Reuben!" she encouraged me.

"Who's Reuben?" I asked. Actually, it was probably closer to, "Uh, like, who's Reuben?"

"It's this really great sandwich, you'll love it!" she said as she raced up to the counter and placed the order.

As we waited for our order to be ready, I fiddled with the red plastic "12" that an angry kid obviously not named Rose handed my mom. If his name was Rose, he had problems bigger than wearing his grandma's shoes. Then again, he had a chain of Portland delis, so life couldn't be that bad for "Rose."

"So, like, what is in this sandwich?" I asked begrudgingly. Dude, Orange Julius was right next door!

"Well, first they take rye bread..." I could hear the excitement building in my mom's voice, "and then they slather it with Thousand Island dressing. They put sauerkraut, Swiss cheese and pastrami on top, and then they grill it, so it all gets melted and delicious."

Again, the same thoughts raced through my head as had a few years prior during our baby-making talk.

"What?! That sounds totally grody! Why would anyone want to do that? Have *you* done that before? I'm never doing that! Yuck!"

Rye bread? Isn't that the bread with all the little seeds? And I wouldn't touch Thousand Island dressing even if it were the only option at the school cafeteria salad bar. Only the gross boys picked Thousand Island. Sauerkraut was just plain scary, Swiss cheese tasted like feet, and I always peeled off the peppery edge of pastrami and discarded it in a spicy pile in the bottom of my lunch bag with that overripe banana that made my whole sandwich taste funky.

But when "Rose" brought out our sandwich, its golden crust glistening, cheese oozing out the sides and a melded mass of salty, sweet and spicy fillings, steamy and harmonious in their unification, it was lust at first bite. All preconceived notions that I had about how gross it would be were gone, and suddenly I could see myself enjoying this bliss time and time again.

It's somewhat fitting that as my birthdays passed, and I eventually met a boy, got married and got pregnant, my love for this sandwich reached a whole new level. I ate a Reuben nearly every day that I was pregnant with Gigi and Lulu, and my "last supper" before both trips to the hospital to give birth was in fact a Reuben.

Like my perspective on sex, my Reuben has changed quite a bit over the years, especially since having kids. I still enjoy sharing it with someone I love, and I don't get it nearly as often as I'd like, but at least there's always my birthday.

Use the Thousand Island Dressing on salads, as a dip for fresh vegetables or a sauce for Tofu Fun Nuggets (p. 131).

INGREDIENTS

1 package tempeh bacon (i.e., Lightlife Fakin' Bacon)

2 tablespoons vegan margarine (i.e., Earth Balance), melted

8 slices rye bread

1 cup non-dairy Swiss or mozzarella (i.e., Daiya mozzarella shreds) or organic Swiss cheese slices

1⅓ cups sauerkraut

Thousand Island Dressing:

½ cup non-dairy or organic mayonnaise (i.e., Vegenaise)

¼ cup organic ketchup

2 tablespoons sweet pickle relish

DIRECTIONS

1　Prepare bacon according to package directions and set aside.

2　Melt margarine and lightly brush onto one side of each slice of bread.

3　In a small bowl, combine mayonnaise, ketchup and relish and set aside.

4　Place a large skillet over medium-high heat. Put one slice of bread, margarine side down, in the bottom of the skillet.

5　Top bread with ¼ cup or slice of cheese of your choice, and then ⅓ cup of sauerkraut. Break three slices of bacon to fit on bread and then place on top of sauerkraut.

6　Put a generous 2 tablespoons of dressing on the non-margarine side of another slice of bread and put it facedown on top of the bacon.

7　Grill sandwich for several minutes on each side, until cheese is melted and bread is golden brown. Repeat for remaining sandwiches.

NUTRITION INFORMATION PER SERVING: 421 calories, 21 g total fat, 4 g saturated fat, 0 mg cholesterol, 905 mg sodium, 48 g carbohydrates, 6 g fiber, 12 g protein

beyond Pea B and J

hugh jass salad

Makes 1, well, Hugh Jass Salad

I'M A BIT EMBARRASSED TO ADMIT THAT I EAT PRETTY MUCH THE SAME thing for lunch every day, a Hugh Jass Salad.

In other words, I'm embarrassed by my Hugh Jass. As a food blogger, it eventually got to be where I was posting pictures of my Hugh Jass on the internet every day, receiving comments like, "Wow! That Hugh Jass looks amazing!" or "I'd kill for a Hugh Jass like yours!" Eventually, bloggers and readers started building their own Hugh Jasses and giving me credit for the inspiration of their oversized, slightly profane creations. I know you are so proud, Mom.

Ironically, the beauty of a Hugh Jass, aside from its sheer size, is the fact that the possibilities are endless, and that I can have a Hugh Jass 365 days a year, and almost never eat the same exact thing twice. I've found no better way to combine a variety of fresh vegetables, healthy fats and lean protein in a satisfying and stimulating meal. So today I stand proud and shout to the world, "I love my Hugh Jass!"

INGREDIENTS

3 cups base greens, washed, torn and dried (choose any variety):
  romaine
  spinach
  field greens
  arugula
  cabbage

2 to 3 cups fresh vegetables, washed and chopped (choose any variety):
  broccoli
  carrots
  cucumbers
  bell peppers
  snow peas
  sprouts
  tomatoes
  pickled beets
  corn

4 ounces protein (choose one):
  precooked tofu
  precooked tempeh
  precooked seitan
  precooked veggie burgers, meatless
    meatballs, veggie dogs or
    sausages, chickpeas, black or
    pinto beans

2 tablespoons to ¼ cup salad dressings (choose one or more):
  lemon juice
  olive oil
  Bragg Liquid Aminos
  hummus
  organic barbecue sauce
  mustard
  homemade or store-bought
    dressings

2 tablespoons to ¼ cup toppings (choose one or more):
  nuts
  seeds
  dried fruits
  diced avocado
  Croutons (p. 109)

Don't be afraid to try different combinations to "beef up" your salad. The key to be satisfied with a meal-sized salad is to add components that have heartiness: lean veggie protein sources, healthy fats and a variety of textures. Just make sure you start with a bowl big enough to contain your Hugh Jass.

DIRECTIONS

1 In a large mixing bowl, place base greens. Layer vegetables and protein on top of greens.

2 Top with dressings and toppings of your choice, grab a fork and dig into that Hugh Jass.

NUTRITION INFORMATION PER SERVING (for spinach, vegetables, tofu, lemon juice, olive oil, dried fruits): 382 calories, 12 g total fat, 2 g saturated fat, 0 mg cholesterol, 195 mg sodium, 55 g carbohydrates, 13 g fiber, 27 g protein

spicy african peanut slow cooker soup

Makes 4 large bowls

SOMEWHERE IN BETWEEN APPLIANCE HEAVEN AND HELL LIES THE CUP-
board above our refrigerator. Unlike the garage, you don't need to leave the
room or enter the elements to access its contents, but you do need to kick
off your heels and grab a chair to stand on before you can get to the home
of lesser-used gadgets. Right behind the rice cooker and to the left of the ice
cream maker rests the cumbersome Crock-Pot. Said to be the working mom's
dream, the slow cooker is ideal for tenderizing meat. Though I am technically
a stay-at-home mom, it's a rare day that I stay at home, and though I don't
cook meat, I do like to "set it and forget it." This hearty, delicious recipe has
me rethinking where to store my kitchen equipment. Get excited, slow cooker,
you're going places.

You can also
make this soup
on the stove top,
if you don't have
a slow cooker or
just can't remem-
ber where you
stashed it. Simply
put all ingredi-
ents in a large
pot and bring to
a simmer for 20
to 30 minutes.

INGREDIENTS

1 14-ounce can chickpeas, drained
and rinsed

1 sweet potato, cubed
(approximately 1 cup)

1½ teaspoons curry powder

½ to ¾ teaspoon garam masala
(depending on how spicy you like it)

1 teaspoon cumin

1 tablespoon minced ginger

2 teaspoons minced garlic

sweetener to taste (organic sugar
or stevia)

dash of cinnamon

1 14-ounce can organic fire-roasted
tomatoes, in juice

1 14-ounce can light coconut milk

2 cups vegetable stock

2 tablespoons natural peanut butter

½ cup red lentils, drained and rinsed

Garnishes:
chopped cilantro, chopped
peanuts, dairy-free or organic sour
cream, or organic plain yogurt

DIRECTIONS

Combine all ingredients in a Crock-Pot and set on high for about a half an
hour, and then switch to low for an additional 3 to 4 hours. Serve and pass
garnishes at the table.

NUTRITION INFORMATION PER SERVING: 285 calories, 15 g total fat, 11 g saturated fat,
0 mg cholesterol, 345 mg sodium, 31 g carbohydrates, 10 g fiber, 11 g protein

panzanella salad

Makes 4 entrée-sized salads

I NOT-SO-SECRETLY HAVE A HUGE GIRL CRUSH ON GIADA DELAURENTIS. I love the way she puts Nutella in everything. I love the way "Parmigiano Reggianno" rolls off her tongue. I love how casually and gracefully she moves about the kitchen as she's preparing a gourmet spread for an outdoor gathering of friends who happen to be arriving just as she's putting the finishing touches on everything. I can't imagine her shrieking at her husband to stall getting the door because she just dropped half of the rolls on the floor and the guests can't see her replating them. Plus she'd probably serve croissants, anyway. And she'd pronounce it: "qua-sonz!"

Our similarities end with our quite large and voluptuous...heads. Giada obviously likes her fresh mozzarella and her prosciutto. I still take inspiration from her recipes, though, and I certainly could take a cue from her on keeping my cool as a hostess. I love the idea of adding bread and grilled vegetables to an everyday salad and calling it by an Italian name: "panzanella." My version is hearty enough for bigger appetites and glamorous enough for entertaining. As a bonus, the bread's right in it, so you don't have to worry about where your roll has been.

INGREDIENTS

1 bunch asparagus, trimmed

1 tablespoon olive oil

salt and pepper to taste

1 small lemon

1 head romaine lettuce, washed and torn into bite-sized pieces

1 cup cherry tomatoes, halved

¼ cup fresh basil, chopped

½ cup green olives, sliced

1 cup non-dairy or organic mozzarella cheese, cut into 1-inch cubes

2 meat-free Italian sausages (i.e., Tofurky or field roast), cooked according to package directions and cut into bite-sized pieces (optional)

1 batch Balsamic Vinaigrette (p. 127)

1 batch Croutons (p. 109)

DIRECTIONS

1   For asparagus, preheat oven to 400 degrees.

2   Place asparagus on a baking sheet and drizzle with olive oil. Season with salt and pepper and toss asparagus until it is evenly coated. Roast until spears are lightly browned, but still crisp tender, approximately 12 to 15 minutes. Zest and juice the lemon and top asparagus with both. Set aside.

3   In a large bowl, combine romaine, tomatoes, basil, olives, cheese, sausages, if using, and Croutons. Cut asparagus into 1- to 2-inch pieces and add to salad.

4   Toss salad with Balsamic Vinaigrette and serve.

NUTRITION INFORMATION PER SERVING: 212 calories, 13 g total fat, 2 g saturated fat, 0 mg cholesterol, 776 mg sodium, 20 g carbohydrates, 6 g fiber, 9 g protein

pea POINTS

If making this salad ahead of time, wait to add the dressing and croutons until just before serving to prevent any unwanted sogginess.

beyond Pea B and J

skinny elvis sandwiches

Makes 4 sandwiches

IT'S COMMON KNOWLEDGE THAT ELVIS'S FAVORITE SANDWICH WAS peanut butter and banana. But was it really? Do you think if he were alive today (sorry, Grandma, I'm not buying that you saw him at Walgreens last week), Elvis would confirm our long-held belief, or would he say, "You know, Little Mama, those bananas always got a bit mushy"? I made over The King's favorite sandwich for my "king," with whole grain bread, the healthy fats of almond butter and antioxidant-rich strawberries. When I place this juicy, creamy sandwich in front of Pea Daddy, he always says, "Thank you…thank you very much."

INGREDIENTS

8 slices whole wheat or sprouted grain bread (i.e., Ezekiel 4:9)

½ cup almond butter (creamy or crunchy)

1 tablespoon cinnamon, divided

1 pint fresh strawberries, cleaned and sliced

1 tablespoon melted vegan margarine (i.e., Earth Balance) or cooking spray

DIRECTIONS

1   Place a nonstick skillet over medium-high heat. If not using margarine, spray pan with cooking spray.

2   Slather four slices of bread with 2 tablespoons of almond butter each and sprinkle with several dashes of ground cinnamon. Layer strawberries on top of almond butter and top sandwich with an additional slice of bread.

3   If using margarine, lightly brush both sides of the sandwich with the melted margarine using a pastry brush and then place sandwich in the heated skillet.

4   Grill for several minutes on each side, until bread is golden brown and almond butter is melted.

NUTRITION INFORMATION PER SERVING: 368 calories, 16 g total fat, 3 g saturated fat, 0 mg cholesterol, 289 mg sodium, 35 g carbohydrates, 6 g fiber, 12 g protein

pea POINTS

Unlike peanut butter, almond butter has no saturated fat and has healthy doses of magnesium and potassium. Creamy or crunchy, roasted or raw, almond butter comes in many delicious varieties so find the one that you like best. We like it roasted, crunchy and spread thick!

79

beyond Pea B and J

thai crunch salad (page 82)

thai crunch salad

Makes 4 entrée-sized salads

pea POINTS

For a time-saving shortcut, buy seasoned, precooked organic tofu found in the refrigerated section of your natural foods store. Simply cube the tofu and toss it in with the salad.

IF WE THOUGHT PLANNING A DATE NIGHT WAS HARD AFTER HAVING TWO kids, we had no idea how hard it could be until we went veg. Our old date night looked a lot like this:

1. Squeeze into pair of jeans bought in a Juniors department during law school. Find shirt long enough to cover bulging zipper and a "rise" that seems to be getting lower at the same rate as my breasts.

2. Pack an evening bag, not for my lipstick and compact, but for Gigi and Lulu's pj's, blankies, dolls and dolls, pj's, dolls, blankies and dolls' dolls. Funny how I can't spring for new jeans, but the dolls have dolls, and those dolls have some really cute jeans.

3. Drop girls off at Mimi and Poppy's house.

4. Go jeans shopping.

5. Order by phone and have the pizza, salad and wine waiting at the restaurant for dangerously fast consumption to ensure we still make bedtime.

6. Pray new jeans still fit.

While there are many great vegetarian and vegan restaurants with fantastic options, I still am not a fan of jeans. I like to be able to enjoy a date night in my yoga pants. I make a mean Barbecue Chickpea Pizza (p. 169) that is reliably close to Pea Daddy's old favorite, and this salad of crunchy textures and Asian flavors is even better than the original, much like today's variety of date night.

We'll wear the girls out at the park, put them to bed early, change out of our jeans and have a date night at home. While the pizza is baking, we lovingly debate why my movie choice is far superior than anything starring "The Rock." As easy as this salad is to make, there just still may be time on our date night to do that thing that made us parents in the first place.

INGREDIENTS

1 head napa cabbage, cut into ¼-inch strips

1 head romaine lettuce, cut into ¼-inch strips

2 large carrots, peeled and julienned

2 bunches scallions, thinly sliced

1 large English cucumber, julienned

1 large bunch cilantro, chopped

2 cups cooked, shelled edamame

1 cup roasted peanuts

4 servings Teriyaki Tofu (p. 161) (optional)

1 cup Almond Ginger Dressing (p. 122) or store-bought organic Asian dressing of your choice

1 cup crispy wonton strips (optional)

DIRECTIONS

1 Place cabbage, lettuce, carrots, scallions, cucumber, cilantro, edamame and peanuts in a very large mixing bowl and toss to mix. If using, cut tofu into ½-inch cubes and add to mixing bowl.

2 Pour Almond Ginger Dressing into bowl and toss to mix thoroughly. Gently toss in crispy wonton strips, if using. Serve immediately.

NUTRITION INFORMATION PER SERVING: 425 calories, 18 g total fat, 3 g saturated fat, 0 mg cholesterol, 203 mg sodium, 43 g carbohydrates, 16 g fiber, 18 g protein

beyond Pea B and J

fresh waldorf salad

Makes 4 to 6 side salad servings or 2 to 4 entrée-sized salads

SOMETHING ABOUT A WALDORF SALAD JUST SCREAMS "OLD" TO ME.
Maybe it's the raisins. Maybe it's the image of a little blue-haired lady bringing a Tupperware full of the mayonnaise-y salad to a church potluck. Maybe it's the fact that the name Waldorf instantly reminds me of the old puppet guys sitting in the balcony of *The Muppet Show* throwing one-liners at Fozzie Bear. No matter what the case, this version of the classic salad is much fresher (and in my opinion, much tastier) than its ancient predecessors. The raisins have been swapped for grapes and the mayo's been swapped for a light, dairy-free lemon dressing. This salad is great as a side dish or can be made heartier with some precooked tofu or crumbled tempeh. The options are so endless, this salad will never get old.

Stuff this salad into whole wheat pitas or La Hacienda de Peas Tortillas (p. 102) for a fresh and crunchy sandwich option.

INGREDIENTS

Dressing:
¼ cup vegan mayonnaise (i.e., Vegenaise)

2 tablespoons fresh lemon juice

salt and pepper to taste

¼ cup plain non-dairy or organic yogurt

Salad:
1 large head romaine lettuce, washed, trimmed and cut into bite-sized pieces

1 cup organic grapes, washed and halved

1 organic apple, any variety (Fuji and Granny Smith are our favorites), washed and chopped into bite-sized pieces

½ cup roasted pecans

DIRECTIONS

Whisk together mayonnaise, yogurt, lemon juice, and salt and pepper. Add lettuce, apple and grapes and toss until evenly coated. Chill until serving. Top with roasted pecans.

NUTRITION INFORMATION PER SERVING (for 4 entrée-sized salads): 230 calories, 13 g total fat, 1 g saturated fat, 0 mg cholesterol, 135 mg sodium, 22 g carbohydrates, 6 g fiber, 5 g protein

Peas on the Side: Snacks, Sides and Sauces

3

SIDE DISHES AREN'T JUST AFTERTHOUGHTS FOR ME, THEY MAKE A MEAL special. A Crack Wrap is just a quesadilla without some Crazy Good Hummus on it. A Hugh Jass Salad is just a big bowl of lettuce without a tasty dressing.

And as for what to eat in between meals? A little healthy nosh never spoiled anyone's appetite.

Many of the recipes in this chapter have replaced packaged foods that our family had pseudo-addictions to: bottled salad dressings, barbecue sauce, croutons and even French fries. Since I make them at home now, I control what goes in them, using fresh, natural ingredients and no additives or preservatives. I feel so good about these sides that sometimes they turn into the main dishes.

fruit skewers with "cheesecake" dip

Makes 6 to 8 servings

IT TOOK ONLY ONE WEEK OF GIGI'S PRESCHOOL TO REALIZE what a weird mother I really am. There were other mothers who drove SUVs in asymmetrical bobs and yoga pants. In fact, this is a requirement for mothers in their mid-thirties, not ready for minivans, frosted crop cuts and Dockers, but far too old for Jettas, extensions and skinny jeans. By all appearances, I blended in. My eccentricities sprouted their organic heads when I began to see what other parents were bringing to celebrate their child's fifth birthday.

In the first week alone, there were two "Birthday Celebrations." I never was a math genius, but with eighteen kids in a class that meets three days a week, minus breaks, holidays and vacations, it meant pretty much every day was a Birthday Celebration. And since Gigi's birthday was a mere eight months and eighteen days away from the start of the school year, after each celebration, she was intent on planning her Birthday Celebration menu. My vision of healthy, nutritious treats was clouded by the fructose fog, or rather tornado, that swept through preschool at 11:30 a.m. almost every day.

A twelve-foot roll of Bubble Tape.

An entire sleeve of mini chocolate donuts.

A Handi-Snacks pack of cookie breadsticks with frosting for dipping.

And my personal favorite: a full-sized, six-cookie "Fun Pack" of Oreos.

Yes, my daughter was handed six cookies' worth of trans-fat-filled fun. My daughter has yet to develop any sort of tolerance for junk food, meaning I was confined to a car with Sugarlips McSweetypants for a torturous thirty-five-minute drive home. Once there, I had to convince her to stop jumping from the windowsill to the ottoman with her shirt pulled over her head. The green smoothie I had planned for lunch seemed futile now.

The fact that I had over eight months to come up with a healthy alternative that wouldn't make Gigi the object of preschool ridicule worked in my favor. I also had the benefit of the looser food-handling rules of a private school, permitting me to bring a semi-homemade snack rather than being confined to the "food" found in the bakery or middle aisles of the grocery store.

Luckily, given the way Gigi and Lulu fight for a little prime produce drawer pilfering, I knew fruit was my friend. Finding an attractive serving method was the next step. It probably doesn't speak well of me as a mother that I would rather have my children play with sharp sticks than eat a store-bought cupcake. Not only will I put my own child at risk, but I will endanger a roomful of preschoolers with their five-year-old ability to reason, their not fully developed hand-eye coordination and their pent-up aggression at getting slighted on artificially shortening-piped sponge cake. Still, it was a risk I was willing to take.

When I brought the skewers and cheesecake dip to Gigi's preschool class, I was prepared for the worst, but pleasantly surprised. No one complained. No one was stabbed. No one crawled under their desk, barked like a dog and used their pencils as drumsticks to perform a killer drum solo against the heating vent. More important, Gigi's teacher came up and thanked me with such enthusiasm and gratitude for bringing something not completely devoid of nutrition that I began to wonder if she wasn't rethinking her marriage. What can I say? I've got a nice haircut and some great-fitting yoga pants.

pea POINTS

The cheesecake dip is so delicious, it can be eaten on its own. Layer it in parfait glasses with berries or banana slices, and top with granola, toasted coconut or graham cracker crumbs.

INGREDIENTS

Bamboo skewers:

2 cups organic grapes

2 cups organic strawberries, halved or quartered, depending on size

2 cups fresh pineapple, cut into chunks

2 cups kiwi, peeled and cut into chunks

bamboo skewers

Dip:

4 ounces non-dairy cream cheese (i.e., Tofutti Better Than Cream Cheese) or organic cream cheese

½ cup extra-firm silken tofu

½ cup organic powdered sugar

½ teaspoon ground ginger

2 tablespoons fresh squeezed orange juice

orange zest for garnish

DIRECTIONS

1 Skewer prepared fruit and refrigerate until serving.

2 For dip, combine all ingredients in a food processor or blender until smooth. Adjust amount of orange juice until dip has reached desired consistency. Garnish with orange zest. Cover and chill until serving.

NUTRITION INFORMATION PER SERVING (for 8 servings): 141 calories, 2 g total fat, 1 g saturated fat, 4 mg cholesterol, 39 mg sodium, 30 g carbohydrates, 3 g fiber, 3 g protein

peas on the side

my kind of bar

Makes 12 bars

MY MOM CALLED ME AT THE CRACK OF DAWN ONE MORNING, WHICH means that either somebody has died or she sat on her cell phone on the way to work. "What is it?" I asked, bypassing any formalities. Her tone immediately put me at ease (and simultaneously annoyed me for the unnecessary heart palpitations I was experiencing), as she asked, "Do you think you could make over my favorite nutrition bar?" Only she didn't say "favorite nutrition bar." But I bet if you make these, you'll know exactly what *kind* of bar she's talking about. Or you can call me and ask. Just wait until after 9:00 a.m.

Keep these bars in the fridge to maintain their firmness and crunch for up to a week.

INGREDIENTS

2 tablespoons flaxseeds (or approximately 3 tablespoons ground)

½ cup maple syrup, agave, honey or a combination thereof

1 teaspoon salt

1 cup roasted whole almonds, coarsely chopped

½ cup chopped dried apricots

1 cup unsweetened shredded coconut

DIRECTIONS

1   Preheat oven to 350 degrees.

2   Grind flaxseeds and combine in a small bowl with syrup, agave or honey and salt.

3   Coarsely chop almonds and apricots and add them to a large bowl along with coconut. Pour in flax mixture and toss until evenly coated.

4   Spread batter into an 8 × 8-inch pan that has been coated with cooking spray. Bake for approximately 25 minutes, until bars are slightly browned and edges are crisp. Let pan cool only slightly before cutting into bars. If they are too warm, they will not stay together (though you can press them back together), but if they are too cool, you'll have to chisel them out.

NUTRITION INFORMATION PER SERVING: 165 calories, 9 g total fat, 4 g saturated fat, 0 mg cholesterol, 199 mg sodium, 21 g carbohydrates, 3 g fiber, 3 g protein

peas on the side

banana chocolate chip millet muffins

Makes 12 muffins

I OFTEN ASK THE GIRLS FOR INPUT IN OUR BAKING ADVENTURES, AND no matter what the question is, the answer is always, "Chocolate!" The day I created these muffins, I had some overripe bananas and a sack of millet staring at me from the cupboard for the millionth time that month. What good is it buying every superfood you've ever heard of if you aren't going to do anything with it but knock it over and send tiny supergrains all over the supermessy counter and the now superhazardous floor? Those little guys are superslippery. Somehow, in a stroke of creative genius, or more likely dumb luck, we all won with this slightly crunchy, sweet and chocolatey muffin. In a word, they're super.

INGREDIENTS

⅔ cup millet

1½ cups whole wheat pastry or white whole wheat flour

1½ teaspoons baking powder

½ teaspoon baking soda

¼ teaspoon salt

½ teaspoon cinnamon

2 bananas, mashed plus 1 banana, sliced

½ cup organic brown sugar

2 tablespoons canola oil

½ cup non-dairy or organic milk

1 teaspoon vanilla extract

½ cup dark chocolate chips

DIRECTIONS

1   Preheat oven to 375 degrees. Line a tin with muffin papers and set aside.

2   Place millet into a food processor, spice mill or high-speed blender and pulse into a fine texture. Pour into a large bowl and add flour, baking powder, baking soda, salt and cinnamon.

3   In a smaller bowl, combine mashed bananas, brown sugar, oil, milk and vanilla.

4   Add the wet ingredients into the dry and stir until just combined. Fold in chocolate chips.

5   Spoon the batter into muffin cups and top with banana slices.

6   Bake for 17 to 19 minutes.

NUTRITION INFORMATION PER SERVING: 217 calories, 6 g total fat, 2 g saturated fat, 0 mg cholesterol, 59 mg sodium, 39 g carbohydrates, 4 g fiber, 4 g protein

The millet gives these muffins an almost cornbread-like texture. For a less sweet version, omit the chocolate chips. Serve the muffins at brunch or as a side for soups or chili.

chewy energy bars

Makes 10 bars

pea POINTS

Play with the mix-ins to these bars to find your family's favorite combinations. We like dried cherries and chocolate chips or dried apples and peanut butter…and chocolate chips. So predictable.

I USED TO BUY MY FAVORITE ENERGY BAR BY THE CASE. I WAS BORDER-line addicted to the cookie dough flavor (though it tasted nothing like cookie dough). I adored the chocolate-dipped candy bar for athletes, or former athletes who have to carpool and don't have time to make a bowl of oatmeal. I'd stash my bars in a cupboard away from hungry little Peas and Pea Daddy. My habit wasn't healthy for my pocketbook at over a dollar a bar. It wasn't healthy for the planet, with each plastic wrapper being thrown in my trash at 3:00 p.m. each day. It wasn't healthy for me…to have to say no to Gigi and Lulu each time they asked for a chemically engineered bite. Unlike my former drug of choice, these bars are made with whole, natural ingredients that you can identify with each tasty bite. I almost don't mind sharing.

INGREDIENTS

2 tablespoons whole flaxseeds (or approximately 3 tablespoons ground)

¼ cup plus 2 tablespoons water

2 cups old-fashioned oats

½ cup whole wheat pastry or white whole wheat flour

1 teaspoon baking powder

½ teaspoon salt

¼ cup organic sugar

¼ cup raisins

¼ cup chocolate chips

⅓ cup maple syrup

½ cup nut butter of your choice (peanut, almond, cashew, et cetera)

DIRECTIONS

1 Preheat oven to 375 degrees. Grind flaxseeds and combine with water. Set aside.

2 Combine oats, flour, baking powder, salt and sugar in a mixing bowl. Stir in raisins and chocolate chips.

3 In a separate bowl, combine maple syrup and nut butter and mix until smooth. Combine nut butter mixture with flaxseed-water mixture.

4 Add wet mixture to dry and stir well. The mixture will seem dry, but keep stirring until fully integrated.

5 Press the mixture into an 8 × 8-inch pan that has been sprayed with cooking spray. Bake for 15 minutes. Allow pan to cool slightly, then cut into bars and transfer to a cooling rack.

NUTRITION INFORMATION PER SERVING: 272 calories, 12 g total fat, 3 g saturated fat, 1 mg cholesterol, 124 mg sodium, 38 g carbohydrates, 4 g fiber, 6 g protein

peas on the side

chocolate chip zucchini bread

Makes 1 loaf

THE ONLY THING MORE OUT OF CONTROL THAN MY GRANDPA'S ZUCCHINI crop is my family's love for chocolate chips. This zucchini bread recipe is thus the ultimate win-win. I get to hack off part of an oversized zucchini and they get a sweet, yet healthy, treat. Gigi likes it with peanut butter on top and Lulu likes it with a little non-dairy cream cheese. I just like that I have one less Squashzilla in my fridge. You can double the recipe and make two loaves at a time. Don't worry about using up all the zucchini. There'll be plenty more where that came from.

pea POINTS

This extra-moist bread keeps best in the fridge. Reheat or toast a slice from the fridge for that straight-out-of-the-oven taste.

INGREDIENTS

2 ½ cups whole wheat pastry or white whole wheat flour

¾ teaspoon salt

1 ½ teaspoons baking powder

1 teaspoon baking soda

2 teaspoons cinnamon

⅓ cup canola oil

½ cup unsweetened applesauce

1 cup organic sugar

1 ½ teaspoons vanilla extract

2 cups shredded zucchini

⅔ cup quality dark chocolate chips

DIRECTIONS

1 Preheat oven to 350 degrees.

2 In a large bowl, combine flour, salt, baking powder, baking soda and cinnamon.

3 In a medium-sized bowl beat oil, applesauce, sugar and vanilla. Fold in shredded zucchini and chocolate chips.

4 Add wet mixture to dry and stir until just combined.

5 Pour batter into a prepared loaf pan and bake for 50 to 60 minutes, or until a toothpick inserted in the bread comes out clean. Place loaf on a cooling rack and let cool completely before slicing.

NUTRITION INFORMATION PER SERVING (for 12 slices): 206 calories, 10 g total fat, 3 saturated fat, 1 mg cholesterol, 154 mg sodium, 28 g carbohydrates, 2 g fiber, 2 g protein

peas on the side

soft pretzel twists

Makes 4 large pretzels or 8 small pretzels

WHEN MY MOM TOOK ME SHOPPING AS A kid, it meant loading into the minivan, turning on some Michael Bolton and heading to the mall. I was in awe of the bright, shiny mirage of lit storefronts, well-dressed people toting their shopping bags up and down escalators and toasty, buttery, salt-studded pretzels accompanied by paper cups filled with creamy, orange Technicolor "cheese." These days, I see the mall as a dull, tacky line of overpriced retailers, scantily dressed teenagers toting their cell phones and half-covered asses up and down the escalators…and toasty, buttery, salt-studded pretzels accompanied by paper cups filled with creamy, orange Technicolor "cheese." So when the girls and I go shopping, instead we load into the SUV, turn on Taylor Swift and head to the Target a short mile from our house. Sing fast, Taylor.

But what about those tantalizing yeasty twists of carbs bedazzled with salt? No problem. We make our own.

INGREDIENTS

¾ cup warm water (110 to 115 degrees)

2 teaspoons organic sugar

1 teaspoon active dry yeast (½ a packet)

2½ cups unbleached all-purpose flour (with up to an additional ½ cup for kneading)

1 teaspoon salt

2 tablespoons vegan margarine (i.e., Earth Balance), melted

10 cups water

⅔ cup baking soda

2 tablespoons coarse-ground sea salt

DIRECTIONS

1 Combine water and sugar in the bowl of a stand mixer. Sprinkle yeast on top and let sit until foamy, about 5 minutes.

2 Add flour, salt and melted margarine, and using a dough hook, knead dough for five minutes, adding more flour if necessary, until dough is smooth and no longer sticky.

3 Transfer dough to an oiled bowl and let rise for an hour.

4 Once dough has risen, separate it into four to eight sections. Using your hands, floured if necessary, roll dough into a 24-inch strand (or a 12-inch strand for a smaller pretzel), and shape into a pretzel knot.

Lulu came equipped with a ruler. I'm fighting every urge not to make a joke about her future dating habits right here.

5 Transfer pretzels to a baking sheet lined with parchment paper that has been sprayed with cooking spray.

Gigi had her own visions, including "butterfly" and "flower."

Let's say it's a flower and not something that would disappoint Lulu on a date.

Lulu proudly announced, "I'm going to make mine in the shape of a truck driver!"

Not a truck, a truck driver. Gigi told Lulu to, "Stuff it!" and Lulu obliged.

6 Preheat oven to 450 degrees.

7 Bring water and baking soda to a boil, and drop a pretzel in one at a time, boiling for approximately 30 seconds.

8 Remove pretzel with a spider or a slotted spatula and transfer to a baking sheet that has been sprayed with cooking spray. Repeat for remaining pretzels and sprinkle with sea salt.

9 Bake for 12 to 14 minutes.

NUTRITION INFORMATION PER SERVING (for 8 pretzels): 157 calories, 2 g total fat, 0 g saturated fat, 0 mg cholesterol, 893 mg sodium, 31 g carbohydrates, 1 g fiber, 4 g protein

pea POINTS

You can substitute whole wheat pastry flour for a portion of the unbleached organic flour, for a heartier, healthier pretzel. This is one of those recipes, though, that I usually splurge on with the all-purpose flour.

cowgirl cornbread

Makes 6 servings

MY GIGI IS A BIT OF A FEMINIST. WHEN PEA DADDY IS LISTENING TO A little U2 in the car, she complains that she wants to hear "a girl song." When we go to the store, she always wants to go through the checkout "with the girl." (That made at least one trip with an ambiguous cashier a little awkward.) I've used this to my advantage when it comes to mealtime, though, and often find myself feminizing her food to make it a little more appealing to my little Gloria Steinem. Though this cornbread is "hearty enough for a man," in Gigi's eyes at least, it's all girl.

pea POINTS

Cornbread also makes a great side dish for your favorite veggie chili. Now if only you could find a good veggie chili recipe. (Hint: turn to p. 158.)

INGREDIENTS

1 cup cornmeal

1 cup whole wheat pastry flour

½ teaspoon salt

1 tablespoon organic sugar

1 tablespoon baking powder

½ teaspoon baking soda

¼ cup vegan margarine (i.e., Earth Balance), melted

1 cup non-dairy or organic milk

honey (optional)

DIRECTIONS

1   Preheat oven to 425 degrees.

2   In a large bowl, combine cornmeal, flour, salt, sugar, baking powder and baking soda.

3   In a small bowl or your liquid measuring cup, combine melted margarine and milk.

4   Add wet ingredients to dry and stir just until a batter is formed.

5   Pour batter into an 8 × 8-inch pan that has been lightly sprayed with cooking spray. Bake for 19-22 minutes, or until a toothpick inserted in the middle comes out clean. Serve with margarine and/or honey.

NUTRITION INFORMATION PER SERVING: 187 calories, 4 g total fat, 1 g saturated fat, 0 mg cholesterol, 263 mg sodium, 33 g carbohydrates, 4 g fiber, 6 g protein

peas on the side

la hacienda de peas tortillas

Makes 6 6-inch tortillas

WHEN PEA DADDY AGREED THAT WE WERE GOING TO TRANSITION TO vegetarianism as a family, I knew I would have to pick my battles wisely. Don't get me wrong, I would definitely put my foot down on loading the family up into the Pea wagon and hitting the local KFC for a Double Down sandwich. (Oh, it's as real as a heart attack, kids. Why use buns when you have fried chicken?) But when it comes to the finer points of vegetarianism or even just healthy restaurant fare, there is one food that I almost always let slide: the homemade tortillas from Pea Daddy's favorite Mexican restaurant, La Hacienda Real. Lard? What lard? And isn't lard just an acronym for

LOVINGLY
APPROVED BY
REGISTERED
DIETICIANS?

Maybe not. It doesn't help matters that La Hacienda has an actual "Tortilla Lady" who makes tortillas by hand every day at the restaurant, complete with a viewing window so you can watch her honing her craft. As I stand in front of the Plexiglas window, watching her experienced hands fly over the soft balls of dough in a delicious storm of masa and lard, I feel like I'm ogling a caged animal. Does she feel the weight of my stare and mistake my admiration for scrutiny? I am not suspicious, watching for a sneeze or a cough, *mi amiga,* I am empathetic. We share many things.

Almost every time I step into the kitchen, I hear the screeching sounds of two tiny stools being scraped across our hardwood floor. Initially, there is the argument of who gets the actual stepstool and who has to teeter on top of the Cinderella vanity seat that is hardly large enough to sit on, let alone to stand on with both feet while begging to work as a sous chef. Then the fight turns to prime stepstool placement, who is closest to the workspace, closest to the ingredients, closest to me. As I try to de-escalate the conflict, I feel like a stranger in a strange land, using an unfamiliar language of foreign phrases like "taking turns," "no hitting" and "baking powder is not for eating." While there are many kitchen tasks I'm happy to have assistance with, tortilla making is not one of them, so the girls are resigned to watching. Waiting. Breathing. Begging for scraps, nibbles, tastes and fingerfuls out of the margarine tub.

While I want to free Tortilla Lady from her fingerprint-smudged display cage, releasing her to run free, roam and make soft, pillowy, intoxicating burrito wraps in the wild, Pea Daddy is convinced that if we don't pick up some tortillas to bring home, *la senora* will be out of a job and her dreams of a better life for her and her *familia* will come crashing down. Not to mention that every time we stop by the restaurant, he barely has the warm, foil-wrapped pillows in his hand before the girls are clamoring to try one on the way home where we fill them with black beans, non-dairy cheese, sautéed vegetables, salsa and guacamole. As much as I know that a little of anything LOVINGLY APPROVED by REGISTERED DIETICIANS isn't going to kill them, I'd really prefer if we tried to avoid rendered animal fat.

Were I not willing to compromise, I'd offer up my favorite sprouted grain wraps. They don't exactly melt in your mouth, and are not what you'd call "pliable." They're so full of fiber, we'd have to reconsider our diaper budget as well. So, in the spirit of compromise, I make tortillas myself, with the compromise of using, at least in part, white flour. It does take a little more time than just swinging by the restaurant, and of course, I have the added pressure of mediating the stool jousting match, but I feel better knowing that, at least for one night, the Tortilla Lady has a one less set of eyes on her, and dinner is lard-free. If only every compromise could be this easy.

pea POINTS

Store leftover tortillas in a resealable plastic bag in your refrigerator where they will stay fresh for several days. These tortillas aren't just great for burritos, they make excellent wraps for stuffing with Crazy Good Hummus (p. 116) and vegetables, Fresh Waldorf Salad (p. 85) or simply almond butter and banana slices.

INGREDIENTS

1 cup all-purpose flour

1 cup whole wheat pastry or white whole wheat flour

1 teaspoon baking powder

1 teaspoon salt

1 tablespoon plus 1 teaspoon vegan margarine (i.e., Earth Balance)

½ to 1 cup water

DIRECTIONS

1   Combine dry ingredients in a large bowl. Add margarine and work through flour evenly with your hands until fully incorporated.

2   Pour in water, a few tablespoons at a time, and work in with your hands until a soft ball forms. Knead dough on a floured board for a few minutes until dough is no longer sticky.

3   Divide the dough into 12 balls and set aside to rest for approximately 20 minutes.

4   On a floured board, roll the dough flat (as thin as possible).

5   Place the tortilla in a skillet sprayed with cooking spray over medium heat, cooking until slightly golden and puffed on each side, about 1 to 2 minutes per side. Repeat with remaining dough.

6   Store the finished tortillas in the oven on the lowest setting, covered with clean damp tea towels until ready to use.

NUTRITION INFORMATION PER SERVING: 86 calories, 2 g total fat, 0 g saturated fat, 0 mg cholesterol, 406 mg sodium, 16 g carbohydrates, 0 g fiber, 2 g protein

peas and thank you

pumpkin spice-roasted chickpeas

Makes 4 servings

IT'S OFTEN SAID THAT SOME OF THE MOST INTELLIGENT PEOPLE IN THE world also tend to be the most eccentric. Don't get your hopes up though, Mr. Neighbor with the Overgrown Yard Who Pees in His Sink and Sews Homemade Pockets on His Sweatpants. You, sir, are just crazy.

My maternal grandmother proves the point. While she is most certainly "cut from a different cloth," to this day she remains one of the smartest women I know. "Kinky," as she came to be called due to an unfortunate pronunciation of her last name by my then toddler brother, isn't losing her edge, though she is almost eighty. Step one foot into her dining room and you'll see that within an arm's reach in each direction there is at least one way she is taxing her brain. Crossword puzzles are stacked on top of placemats. An end table houses a Rubik's Cube, already solved, naturally. Her bookshelf is a pastel rainbow of large print edition Reader's Digests from the last two decades, worn from multiple readings. Don't even think of putting your feet on the coffee table; you aren't going to harm the mahogany, but you might dislodge an hour's worth of work on a thousand-piece jigsaw puzzle of a Thomas Kinkade painting.

I can't say that her house was always my favorite place to go as a child. My dad's mom would placate us with Road Runner cartoons, Cheetos and Orange Crush, sending us back home with powdery orange fingers and neon tongues. But Kinky taught us how to knit, fed us "slumgullion" and allowed us to watch only *National Geographic* on PBS. I'd get excited when she would turn the TV on, yet knowing her antenna would pick up only three channels, I prayed with all my might that she would, for the love of God, just stop on *Wheel of Fortune*.

At her house, I grew my love of books and acquired new words. Not out of sheer exposure, as much as necessity. I would rather sit and read "Word Power" out of *Reader's Digest* than watch the mating practices of the hermit crab. My favorite book on Kinky's shelf, though, was her thesaurus, which I would thumb through for hours. My mother would return from her errands to pick me up, whereupon I would say, "Much obliged, Maternal Figure. I deem likely you procured a convivial junket?"

pea POINTS

These are great straight off the pan or out of the fridge for a quick protein and fiber-packed snack.

Kinky's greatest quirks came in the kitchen, though. The kitchen itself was tiny, and after I was about nine, it felt cramped to me. There couldn't have been more than four feet between the small-scale four-burner stove and the single-sided sink. Yet Kinky, who is only four-foot-eleven, navigated the space easily. She had a dishwasher, but she washed all of her dishes by hand and put the racks to another use: as a spice rack. I can't help but giggle thinking of her casually asking if I'd like some cinnamon on my toast, pulling down the hinged door, tugging out the top rack, and plucking out the jar like it was the most natural thing in the world.

Her sink held an empty milk carton that terrified me, with its pictures of missing children. I could be next. But she'd stuff banana peels, coffee grounds and uneaten "slumgullion" into its mouth to take to her garden and help her flowers grow. Her fridge held—among other unusual things like horseradish, sauerkraut and, gasp, Miracle Whip—a large carton of buttermilk for my grandfather to drink tall, thick glasses of with dinner each night. I still shudder thinking of the time I asked to taste a sip. Next to the green carton was a jar of congealed, separated fat, of whose origin and intended purpose I will never be sure. Thank goodness I never asked to sample that.

This is not to say that I didn't enjoy any new foods at Kinky's house. At Kinky's, I'd devour heaping bowls of cornflakes with canned peaches in heavy syrup, doused in honey and whole milk. I'd shovel in platefuls of scrambled eggs filled with sliced hot dogs and drowned in a sea of ketchup. I had my first experiences with mini chocolate donuts, apples with peanut butter, and, be still my palpitating heart, coffee. She'd pour me a mug of hot milk and sugar, topped with a few glugs from the fragrant, steamy pot of adulthood, and I felt as if I suddenly needed a training bra and bikini wax. Still do.

I choose now to overlook the chicken gizzards and fried hearts she prepared and that, as I am reminded quite often, I happily gulped down, double-fisting greasy handfuls so as to not have to share. Yet I gladly acknowledge that it was Kinky who first introduced me to the garbanzo bean. The odd, dry, thin-skinned bean-that-might-be-a-pea was foreign to my palate. My mom's food philosophy was that if she didn't like it as a kid, she wasn't going to fix it for us, which explains the absence of eggplant, squash, curry and chickpeas at our table. Perhaps second-generation mother/daughter rebellion would also explain why those are central ingredients in many of my recipes.

peas and thank you

Whatever the case may be, I fondly think of the times I spent at Kinky's and reflect now on how she and I are so much alike with our book-devouring, wild-life-appreciating, sink-composting, coffee-gulping, chickpea-loving (hyphen-overusing?) ways. Does that make me crazy? Just maybe, but when I make these chickpeas, at least I get the cinnamon out of the cupboard.

INGREDIENTS

1 14-ounce can of chickpeas, rinsed, drained and patted dry

2 tablespoons maple syrup

1 teaspoon canola oil

1 teaspoon apple cider vinegar

¼ teaspoon salt

¼ teaspoon nutmeg

½ teaspoon ginger

1 teaspoon cinnamon

DIRECTIONS

1 Preheat oven to 350 degrees.

2 Combine all ingredients in a large mixing bowl until evenly coated.

3 Spread chickpeas on a cookie sheet sprayed with cooking spray. Bake for 25 to 30 minutes, stirring chickpeas every 10 minutes to ensure even crisping.

NUTRITION INFORMATION PER SERVING: 153 calories, 2 g total fat, 0 g saturated fat, 0 mg cholesterol, 439 mg sodium, 29 g carbohydrates, 4 g fiber, 5 g protein

peas on the side

croutons

Makes 2 cups

WHEN GIGI TELLS PEOPLE THAT HER FAVORITE FOOD IS SALAD, I GET A look not unlike the look I got when she announced to a woman in the grocery store that her little brother Tyrone was on a trip to his home country of Nigeria. She has a creative imagination and an astonishing grasp of world geography. But when she is not making up ethnically diverse siblings, you will often find Gigi munching on a big bowl of spinach, carrots, cucumbers, and tomatoes topped with dressing, and the true clincher: croutons. When a salad is topped with crunchy, buttery bits of toasted bread, no one in our family can resist. Not even Tyrone.

INGREDIENTS

2 tablespoons vegan margarine (i.e., Earth Balance), melted

½ to 1 teaspoon garlic salt

1 teaspoon dried herbs (optional; i.e., rosemary, basil, parsley or oregano)

4 slices firm whole wheat (older bread works great) or sprouted grain bread (i.e., Ezekiel 4:9 bread), cut into 1½-inch cubes

DIRECTIONS

1 Preheat oven to 350 degrees.

2 Mix melted margarine, salt and herbs, if using, in a large bowl. Add bread cubes and toss until evenly coated.

3 Spread croutons on a baking sheet and bake for up to 15 minutes, turning at least once during the baking time, and baking just until bread is crisp and dry. Serve immediately or store in an airtight container for several days.

NUTRITION INFORMATION PER ¼ CUP: 50 calories, 2 g total fat, 1 g saturated fat, 0 mg cholesterol, 93 mg sodium, 7 g carbohydrates, 1 g fiber, 2 g protein

pea POINTS

Try these croutons without the salt and herbs and with a sprinkle of cinnamon and organic sugar. They make a fun topping for a fruit salad, smoothies, or just a sweet and crunchy snack.

peas on the side

lemon rosemary-roasted chickpeas

Makes 4 servings

I AM A CONNOISSEUR OF ROASTED CHICKPEAS. THIS VERSION WAS BORN when I wanted a tangy, crisp version to eat with fresh vegetables, hot pita bread and creamy hummus. While the Pumpkin Spice–Roasted Chickpeas (p. 105) have a warm, sweet flavor that pairs well with Indian or Middle Eastern cuisine, this version is fresh and tart, lending itself to Mediterranean or Italian food. They are fantastic on pasta, salads or just for snacking. As for what variety of wine to pair them with? What do I look like, a sommelier?

Reheat leftover chickpeas in your toaster oven or under the broiler. Just watch them closely so they don't burn!

INGREDIENTS

¼ cup fresh lemon juice

1 tablespoon olive oil

1 teaspoon dried rosemary, chopped

1 teaspoon salt

½ teaspoon freshly ground cracked black pepper

1 14-ounce can of chickpeas, drained and rinsed

DIRECTIONS

1   Combine all ingredients, except chickpeas, in a medium bowl. Add chickpeas and marinate for at least an hour.

2   Preheat oven to 375 degrees. Spread chickpeas on baking sheet and bake for 25 to 30 minutes, tossing several times during roasting.

NUTRITION INFORMATION PER SERVING: 176 calories, 8 g total fat, 1 g saturated fat, 0 mg cholesterol, 874 mg sodium, 22 g carbohydrates, 4 g fiber, 5 g protein

peas on the side

spanish quinoa

Makes 4 side-dish servings

QUINOA HAS GROWN ON ME. I KNEW I SHOULD LIKE IT—IT IS A SUPER-grain, after all, being the only plant-based source of complete protein. Yet I felt a lot like Goldilocks (without the naturally blond, manageable curls) when I tried to find a way to prepare it. When I tried to eat it like couscous, it didn't have the fluff. When I tried to enjoy it instead of oatmeal, it didn't have the bite. But when I tried to enjoy it like Spanish rice? Ahhh…just right. And I ate it all up.

INGREDIENTS

1 cup dry quinoa, rinsed, drained and patted dry

¼ cup onion, chopped

2 cups vegetable broth

½ cup organic tomato sauce

2 teaspoons chili powder

salt and pepper to taste

DIRECTIONS

1   Place a large saucepan over medium heat. Add the quinoa and toast until grains are slightly golden brown, about 4 to 5 minutes.

2   Add onion, broth, tomato sauce and chili powder and bring to a boil. Cover and reduce heat to low. Simmer for 20 minutes.

3   Remove from heat, fluff with a fork and season with salt and pepper before serving.

NUTRITION INFORMATION PER SERVING: 174 calories, 3 g total fat, 0 g saturated fat, 0 mg cholesterol, 438 mg sodium, 31 g carbohydrates, 4 g fiber, 7 g protein

pea POINTS

Toasting the quinoa before cooking it gives it a rich, nutty flavor. Try this dish alongside the Green and Red Lentil Enchiladas (p. 154) or for a lighter, summer meal, on its own with a green salad and Yogi Guacamole (p. 120).

peas on the side

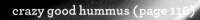
crazy good hummus (page 116)

crazy good hummus

Makes approximately 2 cups

YOU MIGHT THINK IT'S CRAZY TO SIT AND PEEL the skins off an entire can of garbanzo beans. That's where child labor comes in. The satisfaction of freeing the little beans from their skins is on par with popping bubble wrap or peeling Elmer's glue off your palm. But the purpose of peeling the chickpeas is to produce the creamiest hummus you'll ever eat this side of Athens. You'd have to be crazy not to love it.

INGREDIENTS

1 14-ounce can of chickpeas, drained and rinsed (reserve liquid)

2 tablespoons tahini

1 teaspoon salt

2 tablespoons lemon juice

2 teaspoons minced garlic

½ teaspoon cumin

3 tablespoons reserved liquid from canned beans

Optional Garnish:
paprika and/or olive oil

DIRECTIONS

1   Drain and rinse chickpeas and place in a colander. Remove skins from chickpeas by squeezing each bean gently between your thumb and forefinger.

2   Place de-skinned chickpeas in a food processor with remaining ingredients. Process until smooth and creamy.

Variations:
Roasted Red Pepper Hummus: add ⅓ cup jarred roasted red peppers to mix during processing.

Kalamata Olive Hummus: add ⅓ cup pitted Kalamata olives to mix during processing.

Rosemary and Pine Nut Hummus: add 2 tablespoons fresh, chopped rosemary and ¼ cup pine nuts to mix during processing.

NUTRITION INFORMATION PER ¼ CUP: 81 calories, 3 g total fat, 0 g saturated fat, 0 mg cholesterol, 148 mg sodium, 12 g carbohydrates, 2 g fiber, 3 g protein

peas and thank you

butternut squash fries

Makes 4 servings or more (depending on the size of squash)

IT'S REALLY NOT FUNNY THAT MOST AMERICAN children name the French fry as their favorite vegetable. Yet, whenever I think about it, I can't help but giggle. You see, when I ask Gigi what French fries are made out of, she confusedly asks, "France?" I guess the idea of deep-fried potatoes is foreign to her, thanks to this recipe. Chances are, after you make these fries, you and your family will say *au revoir* to those "vegetables" from your past.

INGREDIENTS

1 butternut squash

cooking spray

salt

DIRECTIONS

1   Preheat oven to 425 degrees.

2   Using a sharp knife, cut off both ends of the squash. Cut round end off and reserve for later use. Using a vegetable peeler, remove skin. Carefully slice the neck of the squash into lengthwise planks and then cut those planks into fry-like shapes.

3   Place fries on a cookie sheet that has been sprayed with cooking spray. Spray the fries with a light coat as well and sprinkle with salt. Bake for 30 to 40 minutes, flipping once during cooking time.

Variation:
Curry Squash Fries: combine 1 tablespoon curry powder, ½ teaspoon ground ginger, ½ teaspoon cumin, 1 teaspoon coriander, 1 tablespoon organic sugar and 1 teaspoon salt and sprinkle over fries in place of salt before baking.

NUTRITION INFORMATION PER SERVING: 123 calories, 0 g total fat, 0 g saturated fat, 0 mg cholesterol, 738 mg sodium, 32 g carbohydrates, 9 g fiber, 3 g protein

pea POINTS   117

Butternut squash is rich in vitamin A and is lower in starchy carbohydrates than potatoes. You can find a crinkle cutter at culinary stores and make your squash fries even more legit.

peas on the side

yogi guacamole (page 120)

yogi guacamole

Makes 2 cups

pea POINTS

Even though the fats found in avocados are heart-healthy, I still like to pack extra fiber and protein into my guac. While most versions oxidize quickly once they are exposed to air, this version stays greener longer. This dip will still be fine the next day, if it lasts that long.

ROLL OUT YOUR MAT. CLEAR YOUR MIND from all external thoughts. Let go of the strain and fatigue of everyday life. Open your chakras and focus your third eye. Yogi Guacamole may or may not purify and strengthen your body and mind, but at the very least, armed with a can of beans, we are going to give this dip a good stretch. Namaste.

INGREDIENTS

1 15-ounce can northern white beans, drained and rinsed

1 extra-large avocado or 2 small, pitted, peeled and cut into chunks

2 tablespoons chopped onion

½ cup fresh cilantro

1 tablespoon lemon juice

1 teaspoon minced garlic

¾ teaspoon cumin

½ teaspoon salt

few grinds ground black pepper

DIRECTIONS

Combine all ingredients in a high-speed blender or food processor and pulse until smooth.

NUTRITION INFORMATION PER ¼ CUP: 115 calories, 4 g total fat, 1 g saturated fat, 0 mg cholesterol, 3 mg sodium, 16 g carbohydrates, 7 g fiber, 5 g protein

peas and thank you

fire-roasted salsa in a cinch

Makes approximately 2 cups

I OFTEN TRY TO CONVINCE GIGI THAT BY NOT TELLING ME THAT SHE DID something, like when she failed to mention that she used half a compact full of pressed powder on Pea Kitty's shiny T-zone, it's the same as lying about it. Luckily the equation of an omission equaling a lie doesn't apply to parents. This *is* homemade salsa—it didn't come from jar. The ingredients *are* fresh—I picked out that cilantro and onion at the supermarket a few days ago. The tomatoes *are* fire-roasted—I just didn't roast them. Trust me, no one will know how easy this salsa is to make with its authentic, fresh flavor.... And that's no lie.

When entertaining, I like to make two batches of this salsa, a spicy one for the adults and one without the jalapeño for the kids...and Pea Daddy.

INGREDIENTS

2 14.5-ounce cans organic fire-roasted tomatoes (drained)

1 cup onion, finely diced

3 teaspoons minced garlic

½ lime, juiced

1 teaspoon salt

1 jalapeño, seeded and diced (optional)

3 tablespoons cilantro, chopped

1 teaspoon chili powder

½ teaspoon cumin

DIRECTIONS

Combine all ingredients in a food processor and pulse a few times, until just mixed, but not pureed. Cover and refrigerate until serving.

NUTRITION INFORMATION PER ¼ CUP: 26 calories, 0 g total fat, 0 g saturated fat, 0 mg cholesterol, 297 mg sodium, 6 g carbohydrates, 2 g fiber, 1 g protein

almond ginger dressing

Makes 1 cup

If your leftover dressing gets too thick after refrigeration, simply add a touch of water and remix until you get the desired consistency.

PEANUT SAUCE IS, IN MY NOT-AT-ALL-RESEARCHED OPINION, AKIN TO the ketchup of Asian cuisine. Slap it on just about anything and kids, husbands and vegan mommy bloggers will eat it. This version uses almond butter rather than peanut butter and has the extra crunch of added almonds. It's out of this world on salads, but mighty fine on noodles and stir-fries as well. Gigi is especially a fan. If Lulu eats ketchup on her ketchup, Gigi eats Almond Ginger Dressing on her Almond Ginger Dressing.

INGREDIENTS

½ cup almond butter

½ cup whole almonds
(raw is preferred, but roasted will work in a pinch)

1½ tablespoons reduced-sodium soy sauce

2 tablespoons agave or pure maple syrup

2 tablespoons lime juice

1 teaspoon minced garlic

1 tablespoon minced ginger

½ cup water

DIRECTIONS

Combine all ingredients except water in a food processor or blender. Blend, slowly adding water until desired consistency is reached. Refrigerate unused portion.

NUTRITION INFORMATION PER 2 TABLESPOONS: 97 calories, 7 g total fat, 1 g saturated fat, 0 mg cholesterol, 102 mg sodium, 8 g carbohydrates, 2 g fiber, 4 g protein

everything's better with barbecue sauce

Makes 2 cups

EACH PEA HAS HIS OR HER FAVORITE CONDIMENT. IT GOES WITHOUT saying that Gigi's is hummus and Lulu never met anything she wouldn't put ketchup on. As for Pea Daddy and me, our hearts belong to barbecue sauce. We put it on sandwiches, salads, pizzas and tofu. I've even dipped carrot sticks into a big, sweet, spicy pool of barbecue goodness, and Pea Daddy eats it on sweet potatoes. And though we aren't basting brisket or dousing pulled pork with this sauce, I wouldn't put it past me to brush it on some grilled vegetables, drizzle some on a bowl of brown rice or take a swig straight from the bottle. Each Pea has his or her embarrassing vices, too.

INGREDIENTS

1⅓ cup organic ketchup

⅓ cup molasses

2 teaspoons garlic powder

1 tablespoon vegan Worcestershire sauce

¼ cup apple cider vinegar

2 tablespoons agave or honey

2 teaspoons Dijon mustard

¼ cup plus 2 tablespoons reduced-sodium soy sauce

1 teaspoon liquid smoke

DIRECTIONS

In a large saucepan, combine ketchup, molasses, garlic powder, Worcester-shire, vinegar, agave or honey, and mustard. Simmer for 20 minutes. Add soy sauce and liquid smoke and simmer for an additional 10 minutes.

NUTRITION INFORMATION PER 2 TABLESPOONS: 45 calories, 0 g total fat, 0 g saturated fat, 0 mg cholesterol, 258 mg sodium, 13 g carbohydrates, 0 g fiber, 1 g protein

pea POINTS

I love the combination of barbecue sauce and hummus. Try it on a pita pizza, in a sandwich or on a salad. There's something magical about the spicy and creamy combo that we just can't get enough of, and with this version, you won't be getting the high fructose corn syrup found in most store-brought brands.

lime tahini sauce

Makes 1 ½ cups

WITH ALL THE MULTITASKING THAT TAKES place in our house, Gigi's tutu and Lime Tahini Sauce are the hardest working accessories in Pea Business. The tutu serves as a dance uniform, a fairy princess costume and the one way I can routinely get Gigi to ever leave the house in pants. Jeans alone? No go. Jeans with a tutu topper? Golden. Similarly, this simple sauce serves as a steamed veggie topper, a creamy sauce for fluffy grains and the one way I have routinely topped a salad since I gave up on store-bought. A big bottle is a staple in my fridge and there's nothing I won't put it on. Now if only this sauce could get Gigi to put on some pants.

INGREDIENTS

½ cup water

½ cup tahini

¼ cup lime juice

¼ cup reduced-sodium soy sauce

1 teaspoon minced garlic

agave, organic sugar or stevia to taste

DIRECTIONS

Combine all ingredients in a blender and mix until well combined. Adjust sweetener to taste.

NUTRITION INFORMATION PER 2 TABLESPOONS: 58 calories, 4 g total fat, 1 g saturated fat, 0 mg cholesterol, 181 mg sodium, 3 g carbohydrates, 1 g fiber, 2 g protein

Leftover sauce will thicken up significantly, so add a bit of water to thin it out, as necessary.

cinnamon vinaigrette

Makes 1 cup

MY GIRLS HAVE A THING FOR SALAD DRESSING. IF WE VISIT A SALAD BAR, I have to watch them carefully or they'll start throwing back those little paper cups of self-serve dressing like shots of Cuervo. At home, I can relax a bit and just drizzle a little on top of their salads. That is, of course, unless they want to serve it in little cups so they can use it as a dip for carrot sticks, cucumber slices and bell pepper rings, as they often do with this vinaigrette. Bottoms up, ladies!

INGREDIENTS

1 teaspoon Dijon mustard

3 tablespoons apple cider vinegar

3 tablespoons lemon juice

⅓ cup agave nectar or pure maple syrup

1 teaspoon cinnamon

½ teaspoon ground ginger

½ teaspoon salt

¼ cup canola oil

DIRECTIONS

Whisk together all ingredients except oil in a medium bowl. Slowly add oil while whisking, until dressing has emulsified. Serve immediately or store in an airtight container in the refrigerator for up to 2 weeks.

NUTRITION INFORMATION PER 2 TABLESPOONS: 94 calories, 5 g total fat, 1 g saturated fat, 0 mg cholesterol, 97 mg sodium, 8 g carbohydrates, 0 g fiber, 0 g protein

balsamic vinaigrette

Makes 1 cup

I HEAR IF YOU BUY A BOTTLE OF AGED BALSAMIC VINEGAR, YOU ARE IN for a treat. The vinegar is sweeter, thicker and richer, which makes an exquisite vinaigrette. I hear. If I'm spending $25 on a bottle of something that is aged in oak barrels, it sure isn't vinegar and I'm sure not putting it on a salad. I've found that if I add brown sugar to my vinaigrette, I get the same effect, but keep my money for the finer things in life, like plastic dress-up high heels.

Now those are timeless.

INGREDIENTS

½ cup balsamic vinegar

1 tablespoon brown sugar

½ teaspoon salt

½ teaspoon ground black pepper

1 tablespoon minced garlic

½ cup olive oil

DIRECTIONS

Whisk together all ingredients except olive oil until well combined. Quickly whisk in olive oil until emulsified.

NUTRITION INFORMATION PER 2 TABLESPOONS: 76 calories, 7 g total fat, 1 g saturated fat, 0 mg cholesterol, 96 mg sodium, 2 g carbohydrates, 0 g fiber, 0 g protein

Sure to "Peas" Dinners

4

GOING INTO THIS WHOLE CRAZY NOTION OF FEEDING MY FAMILY nothing but plant-based foods, I knew dinner would be a big deal. I could get away with passing oatmeal off for breakfast, a soup and green salad for lunch and a dairy-free cookie or cupcake for a treat without offending anyone. Dinner is a whole different creature, though. Dinner is the warm, savory smell that greets Pea Daddy when he walks through the door. I want to hear, "Mmm...that smells great," and when we all sit down together to eat, "Can I have seconds?" In theory (or a patriarchal society), a good wife feeds her man "meat and potatoes," and enjoys doing it. There's a turkey on the table for Thanksgiving, ribs on the barbecue on the Fourth of July, and Easter dinner isn't Easter dinner without a ham. Don't even mention the eggs. Yet here I was bucking the system.

If this was going to be a lasting change in our family, salads and frozen veggie burgers weren't going to cut it. Dinner could be a deal-breaker.

The key to coming up with satisfying dinners was to take the dishes that my family already loved—things like spaghetti, enchiladas, burgers and tacos—and tweak the standards to remove the ingredients that I didn't want, but leave all the familiar flavors and textures. When spaghetti still has savory sauce and burgers still have tangy flavor, it's hard to miss a little ground beef. I found that for every seemingly un-revamp-able challenge, there is generally an equally tasty, if not tastier, substitute. Maybe our dinners aren't 100 percent traditional, but the tradition of hungrily passing family favorites around a crowded dinner table is still there. And when Pea Daddy asks for seconds, I can't help but feel proud. It's a done deal.

tofu fun nuggets

Makes 32 nuggets

BECAUSE OF A LITTLE HOUSEHOLD ACCESSORY WE CALL THE "SWEAR Jar," I either have to never stub a toe, spill a cup of flaxseeds on my kitchen floor or leave Lulu unattended with a jar of my expensive face cream, or I have

to come up with a creative way to express my frustration. "Fun nuggets" has become a great stand-in for some far costlier words to utter in the heat of the moment. It's also a fitting name for this recipe, because those nuggets that you get through the drive-thru frankly are just processed sh...Sugar Ray Leonard. Make these nuggets instead, and save your money for more important things, like those moments when there are no creative words to express the calamity of an overpriced facial cream–coated toddler.

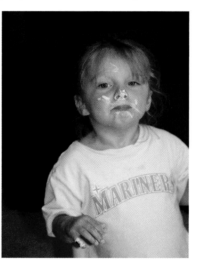

INGREDIENTS

Marinade:

½ cup water

¼ cup reduced-sodium soy sauce

2 tablespoons nutritional yeast

½ teaspoon garlic salt

Nuggets:

1 16-ounce package organic tofu, drained, cut into four equal slabs and pressed according to procedure on p. xxix

1 cup Panko bread crumbs

1 tablespoon flaxseeds, ground

½ teaspoon onion salt

2 tablespoons hummus, either Crazy Good Hummus (p. 116) or store-bought

2 tablespoons water

DIRECTIONS

1   Prepare marinade by whisking ingredients together in a large, shallow dish.

2   Cut each tofu slab into eight equal "nuggets" and place in marinade. Allow tofu to marinate for at least an hour.

3   Preheat oven to 350 degrees and spray a cookie sheet with cooking spray.

4   In a wide, shallow dish, combine Panko, flaxseeds and onion salt.

5   In a small bowl, thin hummus with water.

6   Dip marinated tofu in hummus mixture and then into Panko mixture, coating nugget entirely. Place on cookie sheet and repeat with remaining nuggets.

7   Bake for 25 minutes, flipping once during cooking time. Serve with organic ketchup, Everything's Better with Barbecue Sauce (p. 123), Cinnamon Vinaigrette (p. 126) or Lime Tahini Sauce (p. 125).

NUTRITION INFORMATION PER NUGGET: 28 calories, 1 g total fat, 0 g saturated fat, 0 mg cholesterol, 95 mg sodium, 3 g carbohydrates, 1 g fiber, 3 g protein

peas and thank you

seitan lettuce wraps

Makes 4 entrée-sized servings

THE FIRST TIME I HEARD OF SEITAN, I IMMEDIATELY THOUGHT of the Church Lady. "Could it be, Satan?" I soon discovered that seitan is a great source of protein, and has the texture and heartiness of meat. I created this recipe to replace one of our former favorite restaurant appetizers, and I must say, the flavors and textures are spot on. "Well, isn't that special?!"

INGREDIENTS

Wraps:

1 16-ounce package of seitan, drained

1 6-ounce can sliced water chestnuts, drained and chopped

4 ounces mushrooms, chopped

1 tablespoon organic brown sugar

2 tablespoons reduced-sodium soy sauce

2 teaspoons lime juice

2 cloves garlic, minced

12 romaine lettuce leaves

Dipping Sauce:

2 tablespoons reduced-sodium soy sauce

2 tablespoons lime juice

2 tablespoons organic ketchup

few drops of sesame oil

2 teaspoons garlic and red chili paste

1 tablespoon water

organic sugar or stevia to taste

pea POINTS

Wraps can be messy for little hands, so feel free to serve the seitan over torn romaine lettuce for a salad version or atop brown rice for a hearty stir-fry.

133

DIRECTIONS

1 Spray a large skillet with cooking spray and place over medium-high heat.

2 Sauté seitan until it starts to brown, breaking it up with a spatula as you go. Add water chestnuts and mushrooms to the skillet.

3 In a small bowl, combine brown sugar, soy sauce, lime juice and garlic, and add it to the skillet as well. Cook mixture until heated through and mushrooms are slightly browned.

4 Prepare dipping sauce by combining all ingredients in a small bowl and stirring until well combined. Pour into small cups for dipping.

5 Serve seitan mixture in small bowls with romaine lettuce leaves for wrapping and cups of dipping sauce.

NUTRITION INFORMATION PER SERVING: 267 calories, 12 g total fat, 3 g saturated fat, 0 mg cholesterol, 636 mg sodium, 21 g carbohydrates, 4 g fiber, 23 g protein

sure to "peas" dinners

better than ever black bean burgers (page 136)

MY CHILDHOOD BEST FRIEND LIZ LIVED IN A HOUSEHOLD THAT HAD two big distinctions from mine: They were vegetarian and they were wealthy.

Her father never even batted an eye when we forced him to erect his REI professional-grade tent in their meticulously landscaped front yard so that we could run an "ice cream stand." We weren't hocking ten-cent Otter Pops either. We had higher standards for our first retail experience. Without any objection from Daddy Warbucks, we cracked open his six-dollar box of Milk Chocolate Almond Häagen-Dazs ice cream bars and sold them for twenty-five cents each. Liz's dad beamed with pride at our entrepreneurial spirit.

I'm not quite sure what the motivation was behind their decision not to eat meat. All I knew was that I was happy to stay for dinner when cheese pizza was on the menu, but suddenly had to hurry out the door when a can of Veja-Links was cracked open. If you've never had a Veja-Link, think Vienna Sausages on steroids. The only worse offering for dinner at Liz's house was Curried Eggs on Toast, a vegetarian equivalent to S*%t on a Shingle, but even more worthy of the title.

Häagen-Dazs aside, the most luxurious experience of my indulgences at the big white house across the street was the daily trip through the drive-thru after middle school. Fast food was a rarity for my brothers and me, reserved for when our dentist gave us coupons for free French fries, or when the Book Club at school rewarded my nearsighted, paper-cut-prone beginnings by giving me a free personal pan pizza. Yet here was Liz's mom taking us to fast food row on a daily basis, ordering up fries, milkshakes and cheeseburgers, hold the meat. I'd matured from my ice cream fire sale days enough to know that to pay full price for a bun with condiments wasn't particularly financially sound.

Yet now, I get it: Liz and her family (and I, as their fortunate stowaway) could still enjoy the treat of dining out, the "Made in China" plastic toy, the napkins to fill their glove box with, and the grease-soaked word searches on the side of a colorful carton, even without meat. They could savor the part of the burger that I am convinced is the key to our nation's fast food addiction: ketchup. I've never heard a kid say, "You know, I could go for a nice bloody steak," or "Mom, make sure mine is still mooing," but plenty of kids clamor for ketchup, mustard, lettuce, pickles and tomato on a sesame seed bun with a side of French fries, mine included.

Today, however, my kids reach for a meat-free meal that surpasses any fast food I've ever laid eyes on. When they take a big, juicy bite and respond with a noisy "Mmm…" of approval, I feel like the richest woman in the world. And their friends are happy to stay for dinner.

INGREDIENTS

1 14-ounce can black beans, drained and rinsed

½ cup old-fashioned oats

½ cup chopped mushrooms

⅓ cup onion, minced

1½ teaspoons minced garlic

1½ teaspoons lemon juice

2 teaspoons vegan Worcestershire sauce

2 teaspoons reduced-sodium soy sauce

2 teaspoons cumin

½ teaspoon salt

1 tablespoon nutritional yeast

1 tablespoon tahini

4 whole wheat hamburger buns, toasted

Toppings:
organic ketchup, vegan mayonnaise (i.e., Vegenaise), mustard, lettuce, pickles or tomato

pea POINTS

You can make extra burgers and freeze them for quick weeknight dinners. These burgers have no added fillers or preservatives, unlike the store-bought versions, and we think they taste a whole lot better!

DIRECTIONS

1   Place black beans in a large bowl and mash with a fork until at a chunky consistency.

2   Grind oats into a coarse flour using a blender or food processor and add to bowl with beans. Add remaining ingredients and combine until a thick batter is formed. Place bean mixture into the refrigerator to chill and to allow flavors to meld for at least 20 to 30 minutes.

3   Put a large skillet sprayed with cooking spray over medium-high heat. Using your hands, divide bean mixture into four sections and form each section into a patty. Place patties in skillet and cook for 6 to 7 minutes on each side until the patties are crisp and lightly browned. As an alternative, bake burgers for 15 to 20 minutes on each side in a preheated 350 degrees oven.

4   Serve burgers atop toasted buns and top with additional trimmings, as desired. For the full "fast food" experience, serve alongside Butternut Squash Fries (p. 117).

NUTRITION INFORMATION PER SERVING (with bun): 337 calories, 5 g total fat, 1 g saturated fat, 0 mg cholesterol, 356 mg sodium, 56 g carbohydrates, 14 g fiber, 18 g protein

137

sure to "peas" dinners

thai veggie burgers

Makes 4 large burgers

PEA DADDY LOVES A GOOD BURGER. IN HIS TRANSITION TO VEGETAR- ianism, he's become quite the connoisseur and every time I concoct a new recipe, he updates his personal rating scale. I never thought I would top the Better Than Ever Black Bean Burgers (p. 136), yet when I sat this crispy ginger- and sesame-scented burger in front of Pea Daddy one fateful night and he took a huge mouthful, I watched him begin to struggle. His eyes darted back and forth and he swished the bite around his mouth like it was a vintage port. "It's okay, honey," I assured him, letting him off the hook. "You don't have to choose." As far as I see it, I win either way.

INGREDIENTS

⅓ cup old-fashioned oats, ground into a coarse flour

1 14-ounce can chickpeas, drained and rinsed

2 teaspoons reduced-sodium soy sauce

2 teaspoons lime juice

2 teaspoons sesame oil

2 teaspoons minced garlic

2 teaspoons minced ginger

2 tablespoons natural peanut butter

2 tablespoons chopped cilantro

¾ cup broccoli slaw

4 whole wheat hamburger buns

4 pineapple rings (fresh or canned)

Optional Toppings:
romaine leaves, vegan mayonnaise (i.e., Vegenaise), teriyaki sauce

DIRECTIONS

1   In a food processor or blender, grind oats. Add chickpeas, soy sauce, lime juice, sesame oil, garlic, ginger, peanut butter, cilantro and broccoli slaw and pulse until mixture is combined yet still slightly chunky. Chill mixture for 30 minutes.

2   Coat a skillet with cooking spray or canola oil and heat over medium-high heat. Score bean mixture into quarters and form each portion into a patty. Fry in skillet for 5 to 6 minutes on each side.

3   Toast buns and top with pineapple and other desired toppings. Place finished patties on buns and serve.

NUTRITION INFORMATION PER SERVING (with bun): 352 calories, 8 g total fat, 1 g saturated fat, 0 mg cholesterol, 689 mg sodium, 56 g carbohydrates, 10 g fiber, 15 g protein

pea POINTS

These burgers are perfect for a tropical-themed party. Served with Mama Pea's Margarita Smoothies (p. 11) and Mango Cupcakes with Coconut Cream Icing (p. 213), you can go ahead and redeem that ticket to the Islands...or just send it to Mama Pea. I'll dispose of it for you.

sure to "peas" dinners

mediterranean lentil meatballs (page 143)

homestyle spaghetti sauce

Makes 2½ cups

pea POINTS

I make extra sauce and keep it in freezer-safe containers for several months at a time. I'll pull a container out in the morning and we'll have fresh, homemade sauce just in time for dinner.

IF YOU'VE NEVER MADE HOMEMADE SAUCE, THIS RECIPE IS FOR YOU. Try it in the Almost from Scratch Lasagna (p. 148) on top of Mediterranean Lentil Meatballs (p. 143) or over Tofu Ricotta Gnocchi (p. 144). It's almost as easy as opening a jar, but with the added joy, if you wish, of letting it simmer for hours, rubbing garlic behind your ears, smearing a few splatters on your apron and bringing your thumb and two fingers together to emphasize, "Now 'attsa some tasty sauce!" You'd be right.

INGREDIENTS

2 14.5-ounce cans organic diced tomatoes

1 6-ounce can tomato paste

⅓ cup onion, diced

½ cup fresh basil

2 teaspoons oregano

1 teaspoon salt

¼ teaspoon black pepper

DIRECTIONS

Combine all ingredients in a high-speed blender or food processor and blend until smooth. Pour sauce into a large saucepan and simmer for 30 minutes, stirring occasionally.

NUTRITION INFORMATION PER ½ CUP: 56 calories, 0 g total fat, 0 g saturated fat, 12 mg cholesterol, 506 mg sodium, 12 g carbohydrates, 4 g fiber, 2 g protein

peas and thank you

mediterranean lentil meatballs

Makes 12 large meatballs

THE HARDEST THING ABOUT THIS RECIPE WAS COMING up with a name for these lentil- and Greek-olive-studded spaghetti accessories. As much as they might resemble croquettes, I've always hated that blasted backyard game. And "cakes" just bring to mind frosting, candles and Gigi sticking her fingers where they don't belong. So even though there's not a smidgen of meat in these, it'd be just plain wrong to leave the "meat" out of the title. Just the same, it'd be just plain wrong to serve spaghetti without these "meatballs."

INGREDIENTS

8 ounces precooked lentils or 8 ounces of canned black beans, drained and rinsed

⅓ cup old-fashioned oats

1 teaspoon minced garlic

1 tablespoon vegan Worcestershire sauce

1 tablespoon reduced-sodium soy sauce

¼ cup fresh basil

3 to 4 sundried tomatoes, chopped

¼ cup onion, chopped

1 teaspoon Dijon mustard

¼ cup Kalamata olives, chopped

salt and pepper to taste

pea POINTS

These meatballs also make amazing meatball subs, served on toasted whole wheat rolls, topped with Homestyle Spaghetti Sauce (p. 142) and stuck under the broiler with a sprinkle of non-dairy cheese.

DIRECTIONS

1   Preheat oven to 375 degrees.

2   Combine lentils, oats, garlic, Worcestershire sauce, soy sauce, basil, tomatoes, onion and mustard in a high-speed blender or food processor and pulse until mixture forms a thick, chunky batter. Stir in olives and season to taste.

3   Form batter into 12 golf ball–sized meatballs and place on a cookie sheet that has been coated with cooking spray. Cook for 20 minutes, flipping once during cooking time.

NUTRITION INFORMATION PER SERVING: 60 calories, 1 g total fat, 0 saturated fat, 0 mg cholesterol, 105 mg sodium, 11 g carbohydrates, 2 g fiber, 5 g protein

tofu ricotta gnocchi

Makes 4 servings

MY HIGH SCHOOL BASKETBALL COACH TAUGHT ME MANY CRUCIAL lessons in life: 1) yelling at people for no reason at all can be both enjoyable and motivating; 2) it is both possible and efficient to read while driving; and 3) traditional gnocchi is almost never worth the effort that goes into making it.

Coach Joe was as Italian as they come, and he had the body hair to prove it. When he wasn't yelling at me until a bulging blue vein stood out on his forehead, he was teaching tenth-grade Chemistry in a white lab coat and protective goggles that were worn at all times, even when simply writing on the chalkboard or walking the halls. He looked like an Italian version of Doc Brown from *Back to the Future*, only with crazier hair and crazier eyes. After class, he'd shed his lab coat and trade the goggles for some obscene shorts that more closely resembled my boy-shorts underwear than any sort of athletic apparel. They were bright orange, and were it not for the dense forest of dark, wiry hair that covered Coach Joe from head to toe, I'm sure I would have seen his "gnocchi" up close and personal.

His coaching techniques were unconventional, which is really just another way of saying "terrible." He'd yell my name with such fury and force while I was running and trying to catch a much faster opponent from scoring an inevitable layup, that I would stop dead in my tracks, look right at him and say, "What?!" He'd shoo me off and then proceed to start screaming at me again not thirty seconds later. I finally confronted him about it after a game when he'd made himself hoarse from screaming my first, middle and last name for four quarters straight.

"I'm not yelling your name because you are doing anything wrong."

Come again?

"I'm trying to make a point."

That you remember my name? Oh, like a freshman orientation icebreaker, I get it.

"I want to show the other girls that you can take direction."

It suddenly became clear that if he was going to be able to play me the

sure to "peas" dinners

whole game without being accused of playing favorites by the other girls, or, more important, the other girls' parents, he was going to have to unleash on me publicly to counterbalance any preferential treatment. Logic was as unfamiliar to Coach Joe as appropriate length pants.

The ridiculous gave way to downright dangerous though, when you put Coach Joe behind a wheel. He liked to read, take notes and even draw up plays while he was driving a van full of players to opposing schools. When I was a freshman, the older girls would tell us stories of when our senior guard had to reach over from the passenger seat and grab the steering wheel to prevent the van from careening into oncoming traffic as Coach Joe read a Scouting Report.

Despite his eccentricities, Coach Joe was a giver. His position wasn't paid, and he certainly took a lot of heat, season after losing season. Yet, he'd open the gym any time, day or night, and come help me with my jump hook or my free throws. When my dad was in a car accident, he was one of the first people at the hospital. And when our season ended my senior year and my teammates and I had to say goodbye, he offered to slave away all day in his kitchen making a team dinner of his mother's gnocchi and sauce recipe. I'd never had gnocchi before, and so his description of tender potato dumplings meant nothing to me, nor did the process of peeling, boiling and ricing potatoes and then combining them with flour and eggs to then form by hand enough tiny dough pillows to feed a basketball team. The end result was satisfactory enough, but hardly seemed worth the effort to me, much like volunteering to coach a below par high school girls' basketball team. Thanks, Coach Joe, for giving of yourself, even if it meant getting yelled at, getting an eyeful and getting in close calls in traffic. I think of you every time I make these gnocchi.

INGREDIENTS

1 16-ounce package firm tofu, drained

2 tablespoons fresh lemon juice

3 tablespoons nutritional yeast

2 teaspoons minced garlic

1 tablespoon fresh basil, chopped

½ teaspoon salt

4 ounces non-dairy cream cheese (i.e., Toffuti Better Than Cream Cheese)

¾ cup to 1 cup whole wheat pastry or white whole wheat flour

2 cups Homestyle Spaghetti Sauce (p. 142) or other organic pasta sauce

DIRECTIONS

1 Prepare tofu ricotta by combining tofu, lemon juice, nutritional yeast, garlic, basil and salt in a food processor. When well combined, add in cream cheese and pulse a few times until mixture is creamy.

2 Place tofu ricotta in a large bowl and add ¾ cup of the flour, combining until a soft dough forms. If your dough is too wet, add additional flour 1 tablespoon at a time. Refrigerate dough for 15 to 30 minutes.

3 Turn refrigerated dough out onto a floured board and divide into 4 sections. One portion at a time, roll dough out into a long snake, about 1 to 1½ inches in diameter. Using a sharp knife, cut dough into small gnocchi, about an inch in size. Repeat with remaining dough.

4 While a large pot of water is coming to a boil, transfer gnocchi to a baking sheet. Drop about ⅓ of your prepared gnocchi into the water at a time.

5 When the dumplings start to float to the surface, approximately 1 to 2 minutes, cook for an additional 2 minutes, then remove with a slotted spoon and transfer to a colander to drain. Repeat with the remaining gnocchi.

6 Serve with heated pasta sauce.

NUTRITION INFORMATION PER SERVING: 271 calories, 8 g total fat, 2 g saturated fat, 3 mg cholesterol, 731 mg sodium, 32 g carbohydrates, 8 g fiber, 27 g protein

pea POINTS

Double the batch and freeze a portion before boiling by giving the dumplings a quick toss in flour before packaging. When ready to use, simply add frozen gnocchi to boiling water. The dumplings will still float when they are almost ready, though it will take a few additional minutes.

sure to "peas" dinners

almost from scratch lasagna

Makes 8 to 10 servings

LASAGNA, I'M AFRAID, GETS A BAD RAP FOR BEING HARD TO MAKE.
Lasagna is not hard. Having back labor during your twenty-second hour of
childbirth after four failed attempts at an epidural? Now that is hard. But lasagna is only as hard as you make it.

If you want to make your own noodles, be my guest.
Oven-ready noodles work just fine for me. If you like
homemade sauce, I'll even give you a recipe, but there's
no judgment if a jar is your style. Even the "meat" can
be as effortless as some store-bought crumbles or as
elaborate as handcrafted "meat" balls. You can jazz this
lasagna up with vegetables, or simplify it and leave the
veggies in the salad.

Getting Gigi to put on pants for a trip to the Pumpkin
Patch is hard. Talking Pea Daddy out of buying another
blue dress shirt is hard. Wrangling Blankie away from
Lulu for a much-needed washing is hard. Lasagna?
Hardly.

INGREDIENTS

1 batch of Mediterranean Lentil
Meatballs (p. 143), crumbled or
12 ounces prepared vegetarian
meat crumbles

1 to 3 cups cooked vegetables of
your liking, (optional; i.e., steamed
spinach, sautéed mushrooms,
shredded carrots, broccoli florets,
et cetera)

1 batch of Tofu Ricotta
(see next page)

8 ounces shredded non-dairy
mozzarella (i.e., Daiya mozzarella
shreds) or organic mozzarella cheese

12 oven-ready lasagna noodles or
12 whole wheat lasagna noodles,
prepared according to package
directions

double batch of Homestyle Spaghetti
Sauce (p. 142) or 5 cups organic
spaghetti sauce of your liking

Tofu Ricotta:

1 16-ounce package firm tofu, drained

2 tablespoons lemon juice

3 tablespoons nutritional yeast

2 teaspoons minced garlic

1 tablespoon fresh basil, chopped

½ teaspoon salt

4 ounces non-dairy cream cheese (i.e., Toffuti Better Than Cream Cheese)

DIRECTIONS

1 Prepare tofu ricotta by combining tofu, lemon juice, nutritional yeast, garlic, basil and salt in a food processor or blender. When well combined, add in cream cheese and pulse a few times until mixture is creamy.

2 For lasagna, preheat oven to 350 degrees. Prepare noodles and vegetables, if using, as needed.

3 Pour 1 cup of sauce in the bottom of a 13 × 9-inch baking pan. Layer 4 noodles across the bottom of the pan. Top with ⅓ of the tofu ricotta, then ⅓ of vegetables, if using, and ⅓ of "meat" of your choice. Spread 1 cup of sauce atop of meat and sprinkle with ¼ of the mozzarella.

4 Repeat layering process 2 times, topping with 4 additional noodles, 1 cup of sauce and remaining mozzarella.

5 Cover with foil and bake for 40 minutes. Remove foil and bake for an additional 10 minutes or until cheese is slightly browned. Let lasagna sit for at least 10 minutes before cutting and serving.

NUTRITION INFORMATION PER SERVING (for 10 servings): 312 calories, 10 g total fat, 2 g saturated fat, 1 mg cholesterol, 999 mg sodium, 45 g carbohydrates, 7 g fiber, 15 g protein

pea
POINTS

I love to entertain with this lasagna, especially when hosting guests who might not normally eat meat-free. I make half for the more adventurous grown-ups with spinach, mushrooms, and whatever other vegetables may be roaming around my fridge, and half for the more skeptical kids (and grown-ups) with just sauce and cheese. Either way, the guests are impressed and the leftovers are few.

149

sure to "peas" dinners

baked penne with sausage and peppers

Makes 8 to 10 large servings

ONE OF THE FIRST MEALS GIGI EVER ENJOYED WAS BAKED PENNE WITH Sausage and Peppers. I should add that it was one of the first meals Gigi ever enjoyed *in utero*. Give me some credit. I read and reread enough parenting books to know that the order in which to introduce solid foods is not sausage and peppers, then rice cereal, then strained vegetables. Generally, spicy Italian fare comes between strained vegetables and strained fruits.

Pea Daddy and I went to Disneyland on a whim one weekend in the fall of 2004. We'd been married that January, and though we had the official honeymoon in Hawaii right after the wedding, life since our return had been anything but a honeymoon. In the midst of family divorces, deaths and job losses, we needed to escape and the Happiest Place on Earth seemed like just the place to do it. Maybe it wasn't the most mature thing to do, two stodgy attorneys, leaving our family, friends and employers without our valuable services for a few days while we ran around a theme park pretending we were seven. Ironically, we somehow thought we were less embarrassing than the newlywed couples walking around in bride and groom Mickey and Minnie ears. We were wrong.

Regardless of our immaturity, Pea Daddy and I are a lot alike when it comes to our approach to vacations: go hard or go home. We don't leisurely make our way from sight to sight, taking in the sounds and smells, creating mental postcards to last a lifetime. We get in and get out. We cover as much ground as possible. We are systematic, methodical and efficient, and we have fun, even if it kills us. This approach at Disneyland means that while you may be at one end of the park for It's a Small World one minute, you could very well be at the other end of the park just moments later to beat the line for California Screamin'. There's no time to stop for the parade, a bathroom or to apologize to the woman whose Mickey Mouse Croc you just stepped on. If you stop and watch the parade, relieve your bladder at every whim or concede to rubberized footwear, life passes you by. We are on vacation, damn it.

By day two of our trip, something was off. Our pre-park carbo fueling wasn't sitting right with me, and while normally I've never met a churro I didn't like,

by that second day, I'd met about five that I wanted to un-friend on Facebook and Photoshop out of our photos. After four rides in a row on the Tower of Terror, I wasn't thrilled about dashing across the park to make it to Splash Mountain. I wanted to sit on a bench and eat a Mickey-shaped Rice Krispies Square the size of my head, go to the bathroom and then do it again. If I had a dollar for every time I told Pea Daddy that I "just don't feel right," I'd have ordered a dozen more Rice Krispies Squares.

Our general approach to meals in the park was grab and go, but though I was doing plenty of grabbing, by dinnertime, I just couldn't go anymore.

"So, we've got a Fast Pass for Indiana Jones at 6:00, and another for Space Mountain at 7:30." He started his pitch. "The way I see it," he continued, "that gives us plenty of time to grab a sandwich after the first ride and then eat it while we run across the park for the second."

"Honey," I said in a tone of voice that did not match the endearing term I was using, "I can't do it. If you love me at all, we will find a nice restaurant and just sit and eat." And then I said the words that perhaps may never pass my lips again, "Maybe we can even watch a parade."

As if by divine intervention, we managed to get a spot at a new Italian restaurant in the park, just overlooking the Electrical Light Parade route. I spotted a baked penne dish with sausage and peppers on the menu, and I knew it must be mine. I took the same approach with half a loaf of crusty bread. Somehow the combination of tender pasta, spicy sausage and perfectly cooked vegetables rejuvenated me, made my feet hurt slightly less and, in my mind at least, excused my purchase of a Minnie Mouse T-shirt...and a stuffed Pooh bear. Perhaps it was also by divine intervention that I passed on the red wine that was being poured at nearby tables, because fetus Gigi had already been forced to withstand multiple drops from terrifying towers and screamed-filled loops on coasters.

Not a week after we returned, my shortcomings as a true traveler made sense and life forever changed. So these days, when I plate up a slightly different, yet hefty portion of Baked Penne with Sausage and Peppers for Gigi and she predictably asks, "Do I like this? Have I had this before?" I simply reply with a smile, "Oh yes, dear, you have."

INGREDIENTS

1 pound whole wheat penne pasta

1 package meat-free Italian sausages
(i.e., Tofurky or field roast), sliced into 1-inch chunks

2 bell peppers, assorted colors, sliced

1½ cups sliced onion

2 teaspoons minced garlic

4 cups Homestyle Spaghetti Sauce (p. 142) or other organic pasta sauce

8 ounces non-dairy or organic mozzarella (i.e., Daiya)

fresh basil for garnish (optional)

Don't be afraid of the large yield on this recipe. There's something about leftover Italian food that makes it even tastier the next day.

DIRECTIONS

1 Preheat oven to 400 degrees.

2 Prepare pasta according to package directions until just el dente.

3 Coat a large skillet with cooking spray and place over medium-high heat. Add sausage, peppers and onion until vegetables are tender crisp and sausages are browned, approximately 8 minutes. For the last minute add garlic and sauté briefly before adding pasta sauce. Heat thoroughly.

4 Combine sausage and vegetable mixture with pasta and transfer to a 13 × 9-inch baking dish that has been sprayed with cooking spray.

5 Top with cheese and bake for 25 to 30 minutes or until cheese has melted.

6 Serve and garnish with fresh basil, if desired.

NUTRITION INFORMATION PER SERVING (for 10 servings): 345 calories, 10 g total fat, 2 g saturated fat, 0 mg cholesterol, 969 mg sodium, 54 g carbohydrates, 8 g fiber, 14 g protein

green and red lentil enchiladas

Makes 8 large enchiladas

MY GO-TO DISH FOR ENTERTAINING, EVER SINCE I PRETENDED TO KNOW how to cook as a college student who pilfered half of her ingredients from the dining hall, is enchiladas. My original version might as well have been a block of Velveeta mixed with a jar of salsa, for all its nutritional value. And though my new go-to dish still uses a pre-made sauce and can be thrown together in no time at all, it is far healthier than the shelf-stable version of my past. Now could someone please smuggle me some dining hall tortilla chips, six matching plates and a cake for dessert?

INGREDIENTS

1 30-ounce can of prepared green enchilada sauce, divided

1½ cups water

1 cup red lentils, rinsed and drained

¼ cup chopped onion

1 jalapeño, seeded and chopped (optional)

2 tablespoons chopped cilantro

8 to 10 corn tortillas or La Hacienda de Peas Tortillas (p. 102)

2 cups non-dairy (i.e., Daiya) or organic cheese

1 4-ounce can sliced olives, drained

Trimmings:
non-dairy or organic sour cream, chopped cilantro, shredded lettuce, diced fresh tomatoes and/or Fire-Roasted Salsa in a Cinch (p. 121)

DIRECTIONS

1   Preheat oven to 350 degrees.

2   Bring one-third of enchilada sauce and water to a boil in a medium saucepan. Add lentils, onion and jalapeño, if using, and cook approximately 15 to 20 minutes. Liquid should be absorbed completely and lentils should be tender. Stir in chopped cilantro and set aside.

3   Meanwhile, wrap 8 to 10 tortillas in damp paper towels and microwave for approximately 30 to 45 seconds to soften.

4   Pour one-third of the green enchilada sauce in the bottom of a 13 × 9-inch baking dish.

5   Put several spoonfuls of the lentil mixture into each tortilla and roll, placing the tortilla seamside down in the prepared pan. Repeat with remaining tortillas.

6   Pour remaining green enchilada sauce over rolled tortillas and top with cheese and sliced olives.

7   Bake enchiladas for 20 to 25 minutes, until heated through and cheese is melted. Pass trimmings at the table.

NUTRITION INFORMATION PER SERVING: 278 calories, 7 g total fat, 2 g saturated fat, 0 mg cholesterol, 988 mg sodium, 58 g carbohydrates, 10 g fiber, 17 g protein

pea POINTS

Depending on the spiciness of your enchilada sauce, you may want to omit the jalapeño for less spice-tolerant palates. Removing the ribs and seeds of the jalapeño also cuts back the heat.

sure to "peas" dinners

meaty green bean casserole

Makes 4 main-dish servings or 6 to 8 side servings

SOME SIDE DISHES ARE TOO GOOD TO BE RELEGATED TO THE SIDE.
Chips become nachos. French fries become chili fries. Salads become Hugh
Jasses. Though this traditional holiday side dish is made without that "special"
soup that stays in the shape of the can when you dump it in a bowl, it's beefed
up with fresh mushrooms, vegetarian sausages, water chestnuts and bread
crumbs. You could still have it on the side, but why would you want to?

INGREDIENTS

2 pounds green beans, trimmed and cut into 2-inch pieces

2 tablespoons salt

8 ounces mushrooms (any variety), chopped into bite-sized pieces

1 package meatless sausages (i.e., Tofurky or field roast), diced

2 teaspoons minced garlic

1 8-ounce can water chestnuts, sliced

2 cups vegetable broth

1 cup non-dairy or organic milk (unflavored and unsweetened)

¼ cup plus 2 tablespoons whole wheat flour

2 teaspoons reduced-sodium soy sauce

2 teaspoons vegan Worcestershire sauce

2 slices whole wheat or sprouted grain bread, torn into chunks

1 tablespoon vegan margarine (i.e., Earth Balance)

salt and pepper to taste

1 3-ounce can French fried onions

DIRECTIONS

1   Preheat oven to 425 degrees.

2   Bring a pot of water to a boil. Add green beans and salt. Boil for 5 minutes. Remove from heat and drain, transferring to a large bowl filled with ice water to halt the cooking process.

3   In the meantime, sauté mushrooms and diced sausages in a medium skillet, until gently browned, approximately 6 to 7 minutes. Add garlic during last minute. Stir in chopped water chestnuts.

4   In a small mixing bowl, combine broth, milk, flour, soy sauce and Worcestershire sauce and whisk until well combined. Add mixture to pan and heat until thickened and bubbling. Adjust seasoning to taste.

5   Place green beans in a large casserole dish or a 13 × 9-inch baking dish and pour sauce over the top.

6   In a food processor or blender, combine bread, margarine and salt and pepper.

7   Sprinkle bread crumbs and fried onions over top of casserole and bake for 20 minutes.

NUTRITION INFORMATION PER SERVING (for 4 main dishes): 435 calories, 19 g total fat, 4 g saturated fat, 4 mg cholesterol, 1101 mg sodium, 42 g carbohydrates, 11 g fiber, 24 g protein

pea POINTS

This casserole makes a great holiday meal for carnivores and vegetarians alike. Start with Fruit Skewers with "Cheesecake" Dip (p. 88) and serve with Pumpkin Spice–Roasted Chickpeas (p. 105) and a green salad, then finish with Chocolate Cherry Bread Pudding (p. 230) for dessert for the ultimate holiday spread.

sure to "peas" dinners

tempeh chili

Makes 4 to 6 large bowls

THERE ARE PLENTY OF GREAT VEGETARIAN CHILI RECIPES IN THE WORLD, but few have the heartiness of this one. The tempeh provides the texture and satiety of ground beef, and it keeps the traditional flavors that your family would expect at a tailgate...or tea party. We've got princesses, what can I say? How about, "More chili, please!"

INGREDIENTS

1 8-ounce package tempeh, grated into crumbles

½ cup diced onion

1 stalk celery, diced

1 jalapeño, seeded and diced (optional)

2 teaspoons minced garlic

2⅔ tablespoons chili powder

2 teaspoons oregano

1 teaspoon cumin

1 teaspoon basil

1 14-ounce can black beans, drained and rinsed

1 14-ounce can pinto beans, drained and rinsed

1 28-ounce can fire-roasted tomatoes in juice

¼ cup tomato paste

2 teaspoons vegan Worcestershire sauce

1 cube vegetable bouillon

1 cup vegetable broth

½ teaspoon organic sugar

salt and pepper to taste

Optional Toppings:
chopped cilantro, sliced black olives, non-dairy or organic sour cream or non-dairy or organic shredded cheese

For an even heartier meal, serve this chili atop baked sweet potatoes and pair with a green salad with Lime Tahini Sauce (p. 125).

DIRECTIONS

1 Lightly spray a large stockpot with cooking spray and place over medium-high heat.

2 Sauté tempeh crumbles, onion, celery and jalapeño, if using, until celery is softened and onion and tempeh are slightly browned. Add garlic, chili powder, oregano, cumin and basil and sauté for approximately 1 minute, until spices are aromatic.

3 Add remaining ingredients and bring to a boil. Cover, reduce heat to low and simmer for 20 to 45 minutes to allow flavors to meld.

4 Spoon chili into bowls and pass optional toppings at the table. Serve with, or on top of, Cowgirl Cornbread (p. 101).

NUTRITION INFORMATION PER SERVING (for 6 bowls): 229 calories, 5 g total fat, 1 g saturated fat, 0 mg cholesterol, 536 mg sodium, 34 g carbohydrates, 10 g fiber, 16 g protein

159

sure to "peas" dinners

teriyaki tofu

Makes 4 servings

TOFU HAS BECOME A POWERFUL LEARNING TOOL IN THE PEA HOUSE.
We don't cut it into sugar cube–sized blocks and build igloo dioramas. We
don't sculpt it into a mountain and add vinegar and baking soda to replicate a
volcano. We don't construct parachutes, padded boxes or bubble wrap gliders
to house a block and then drop it from the roof to see if it safely lands on the
ground below. Our tofu lessons are of a philosophical nature: We don't try to
make tofu something it isn't. It's a lesson I take very seriously.

Transforming tofu into something that meat eaters enjoy has admittedly
been a struggle. My list of attempts reads like a scene out of *Forrest Gump*:
tofu meatballs, tofu crab cakes, fried tofu fingers, coconut-coated tofu, tofu
à la king. You get the picture. I tossed batch after batch of unappetizing meals
that were obviously not at all similar to their meat counterparts, and for once,
no one was saying, "It tastes just like chicken."

Eventually, I began to experiment with ways of cooking tofu that accentu-
ated its best features, primarily the texture of a crisp exterior and chewy interior,
and its ability to absorb flavor like no chicken can. I found that my best tofu
successes came when I used simple recipes with tried-and-true techniques for
the best texture and flavor, and stopped trying to dress it up like something it
wasn't. After all, you can put lipstick on a block of soybean curd, but it's still
a block of soybean curd.

These lessons transcended the kitchen and hit me where it hurts, right in
the mirror. I've had naturally curly hair my whole life that I have battled to
keep straight with reverse perms, hot rollers, flatirons and a continuous cycle
of proliferate cursing and repenting prayer. However, no matter how hard I try,
my hair is always less Nicole Kidman and more Phil Spector.

When Gigi was born with a head full of dark, unruly curls, I knew the day
would come when she, too, would start the battle to tame her mane. I pic-
tured her like me, hesitating to walk outside when the humidity was above
2 percent and wearing a rain bonnet if there was even one tiny raindrop drawn
beneath the cartoon puffy clouds in the local television weather forecast.

I thought she would resent me for passing on the cursed curls. I couldn't have been more wrong.

When Gigi sizes up another female, as we all do, she doesn't wistfully look at the glossy, straight-haired blondes and say, "I wish I were her!" Instead, her little eyes scan a group of girls, looking for someone with curly hair. Upon finding her, you'd think she found the left glass slipper that Cinderella Barbie has been missing since exactly eight seconds after she came out of the package. Her eyes light up, her hands fly to her cheeks and she excitedly shouts, "She has brown, curly hair just like me!"

I knew finding someone to identify with was powerful for her, but I had no idea how much so, until the day when I cast my flatiron aside, threw in some product and went au natural.

"Hey, Mama!" Gigi shrieked. "You have brown, curly hair, just like me! You are beautiful!"

So are you, Gigi, so are you. And so is tofu.

INGREDIENTS

1 16-ounce tub of firm or extra firm organic tofu, drained and pressed using technique on p. xxix, and cut into 2 × 3-inch slabs

½ cup reduced-sodium soy sauce

¼ cup plus 2 tablespoons water

2 tablespoons mirin or seasoned rice vinegar

1 teaspoon minced garlic

2 teaspoons minced ginger

2 tablespoons organic brown sugar

2 tablespoons organic sugar

1 tablespoon cornstarch

DIRECTIONS

1 Prepare tofu and set in a wide, shallow dish or pie plate.

2 In a medium saucepan, combine soy sauce, ¼ cup of water, mirin or vinegar, garlic, ginger and sugars. Heat over medium-high heat until sugar is dissolved and sauce is starting to come to a boil.

3 In a small dish, mix cornstarch with 2 tablespoons of water and whisk into sauce. Bring to a low boil and simmer until sauce has thickened.

4 Pour ½ of sauce over tofu and turn tofu until it is completely coated. Reserve remaining sauce.

5 Allow tofu to marinate for at least 30 minutes or overnight.

6 Preheat broiler to high. Place marinated tofu on a cookie sheet that has been coated with cooking spray.

7 Broil tofu for 6 to 7 minutes on each side, so exterior is crisp.

NUTRITION INFORMATION PER SERVING: 233 calories, 10 g total fat, 1 g saturated fat, 0 mg cholesterol, 882 mg sodium, 21 g carbohydrates, 3 g fiber, 19 g protein

pea POINTS

I like to serve this tofu with brown rice and steamed vegetables, drizzled with leftover sauce. You can also use leftover tofu in salads or wrap some up in a La Hacienda de Peas Tortilla (p. 102) with pineapple, brown rice, toasted coconut and baby organic spinach for an exotic wrap.

163

sure to "peas" dinners

chipotle lime tempeh tacos

Makes 8 to 10 tacos

HAVE YOU EVER HAD AUTHENTIC TACOS FROM ONE OF THOSE TACO trucks you see parked on the side of the road, in front of used car lots or on your neighbors' RV pad? Yeah, me neither. I know I'm missing out. I imagine

the ingredients are fresh and the flavors are spot on. Yet I just can't get over eating food that's been prepared in a 1987 GMC van without windows. We still get authentic Mexican fare at home, though, and these tacos are so good, I'm considering selling them out of the back of our SUV. You don't happen to have an RV pad, do you?

INGREDIENTS

Marinade:

2 tablespoons canned chipotles in adobo sauce plus ¼ cup sauce (you can adapt the spiciness by adding more peppers)

¼ cup water

¼ cup lime juice

1 teaspoon salt

2 teaspoons coriander

2 teaspoons cumin

3 tablespoons agave

1½ tablespoons reduced-sodium soy sauce

Tacos:

2 8-ounce packages of organic tempeh

1 package organic taco shells (Garden of Eatin' makes an organic variety)

Trimmings:

lettuce, tomato, Fire-Roasted Salsa in a Cinch (p. 121), olives and non-dairy or organic sour cream and cheese, if desired

pea POINTS

Try the taco filling in burritos, wraps, Tofu Scrambles (p. 45) or on top of a green salad with Fire-Roasted Salsa in a Cinch (p. 121), Yogi Guacamole (p. 120) and baked organic tortilla chips for the ultimate taco salad.

DIRECTIONS

1 Blend all marinade ingredients in a blender or food processor until smooth.

2 Using a hand grater or a food processor, grate tempeh until it resembles the texture of ground beef. Add tempeh to marinade and combine well. Allow to marinate for several hours or overnight.

3 Place a skillet sprayed with cooking spray over medium-high heat and sauté tempeh until heated through and slightly toasted, approximately 4 to 5 minutes.

4 Warm taco shells according to package directions and fill with spoonfuls of the tempeh.

5 Pass desired trimmings at the table.

NUTRITION INFORMATION PER SERVING (for 10 tacos): 235 calories, 8 g total fat, 1 g saturated fat, 0 mg cholesterol, 598 mg sodium, 30 g carbohydrates, 0 g fiber, 13 g protein

sure to "peas" dinners

tried-and-true whole wheat pizza crust

Makes 1 10-inch crust

WE EAT PIZZA FOR DINNER ALMOST EVERY
Friday night. It's a great choice for our mixed family of vegans, vegetarians and control freaks. Those who want cheese can have cheese. Those who want pineapple and pineapple alone can go crazy. Those who want roasted broccoli can…be me. The pizza is like the ocean's tide, a constant, yet constantly changing, depending on our tastes, the season and exactly how many times Lulu has visited the Naughty Corner that day. That's why, whenever I announce pizzas for dinner, it takes one simple question to find out what kind of day I'm having: "On homemade crust?"

When Gigi was born, we started out having pizza every Friday night, and it was never on homemade crust. She was a colicky little thing, screaming like a lamb every night for the two hours before and after dinnertime. Her doctor called her "intense," which was really just a nice way of saying, "Thank goodness these well-child checks are only once every three months." Leaving the house was done only out of complete necessity and so by the end of her first summer, I looked a lot like one of the final contestants on *Survivor*, in desperate need of a haircut, a fresh shirt and a reintroduction to the real world. Yet we had to eat, and thus our Friday night grocery store missions began.

The window of time we had was minimal. In a matter of minutes, Gigi could go from a peaceful, sleeping infant to a throbbing red volcano of

Pizza dough can make a great focaccia stand-in to serve alongside pasta or soup. Simply prepare your dough, but instead of topping with sauce and goodies, use the end of a wooden spoon to make indentations in the dough, give a light brush with olive oil, a sprinkle of sea salt and freshly chopped rosemary. Bake for approximately 15 minutes and cut into wedges.

168

peas and thank you

screams, tears and spit-up. She really could have benefitted from some anger management classes. My main objective was to get in and out of the store before Gigi erupted and I ended up hovering over a public restroom toilet, trying to breastfeed without touching so much as a toilet paper roll holder. My list was meticulous, broken down by aisle, product name and quantity. We'd frantically careen down the aisles, Pea Daddy pushing the cart at a steady jog, and me, tossing items in like a highly caffeinated game of card flipping, praying that at least the essentials would hit their mark.

On a good night, sample stations would mark our path, and Pea Daddy would grab a Dixie cup offering of vitamin water and frantically throw it at his face in hopes that he'd catch a few drops on his parched lips, yet not wanting to slow his pace.

"I think I need to go the bathroom," I'd regretfully admit.

"There's no time!" Pea Daddy would retort. He was right. Next time, I promised myself, I'll wear a Depend.

At Gigi's slightest stirring we'd make the call, like umpires during a rainy game. "That's it, we're done." No time for coupons or receipt scrutiny. They could have charged us $12.00 and a kidney for a jar of peanut butter and we'd have swiped our card willingly. Time was ticking and if we wanted to ever be allowed in Safeway again, we needed to move. As the checker would hand us our receipt, we half expected to hear the national anthem cue up and braced our necks for the weight of our hard-earned medals.

After such a grueling test of endurance and sheer athleticism, we'd come home exhilarated, yet exhausted and hungry. Dinner was thrown together between putting away the fruits of our labor and trying to soothe the savage beast, who had woken up the moment we pushed the cart into the parking lot. Our English muffin pizzas looked more like experiments of a preschool cooking class than the feast we deserved. We didn't care. We were alive.

Thankfully, shopping trips are no longer as insufferable, aside from freakishly large and hard-to-maneuver car-shaped carts. It really takes no time at all, and the payoff is worth the minimal effort. Though I miss the coos and tiny fingers wrapping around mine, I'm grateful we are now afforded the luxury of homemade crust, at least this Friday.

INGREDIENTS

1 teaspoon active dry yeast
(approximately ½ a yeast packet)

½ teaspoon organic brown sugar

¾ cup warm water

½ teaspoon salt

1 tablespoon olive oil

1 cup whole wheat pastry or white
whole wheat flour

¾ cup organic all-purpose flour,
divided

DIRECTIONS

1   In a large bowl, dissolve yeast and brown sugar in water and let sit for
10 minutes, until yeast is foamy.

2   Stir in salt and oil. Mix in whole wheat pastry flour and ½ cup of the
all-purpose flour.

3   Turn dough out onto a clean, well-floured surface and knead in more
flour until dough is no longer sticky.

4   Place dough in a well-oiled bowl, cover with a cloth and put in a warm
place. Let rise for an hour.

5   Punch down dough and form into a tight ball. Allow to rest before
rolling out and topping.

6   Preheat oven and a pizza stone, if using, to 425 degrees. Bake topped
pizza on pizza stone or a cookie sheet lined with parchment paper for
15 to 20 minutes, until crust is golden brown.

Topping Ideas:

Mexican Pizza: top unbaked crust with 1 can of refried beans thinned with
⅓ cup Fire-Roasted Salsa in a Cinch (p. 121) or your favorite store-bought
organic salsa, 1½ cups non-dairy or organic cheese and ½ cup sliced
black olives. After baking, top with fresh tomatoes, non-dairy or organic
sour cream, Yogi Guacamole (p. 120) and crushed organic tortilla chips.

Barbecue Chickpea Pizza: top unbaked crust with 1 can of drained
and rinsed garbanzo beans partially mashed with ⅓ cup Everything's
Better with Barbecue Sauce (p. 123), 1½ cups non-dairy or organic
cheese and ½ cup pineapple tidbits. After baking, top with chopped
fresh cilantro and non-dairy or organic sour cream, if desired.

Apple and Tempeh Bacon Pizza: top unbaked crust with 1 cup
Homestyle Spaghetti Sauce (p. 142) or your favorite store-bought
organic pizza sauce, 1½ cups non-dairy or organic cheese, 1 very
thinly sliced apple and 4 slices of crumbled tempeh bacon.

NUTRITION INFORMATION PER SERVING (for 8 slices): 110 calories, 2 g total fat, 0 g saturated fat,
0 mg cholesterol, 146 mg sodium, 20 g carbohydrates, 2 g fiber, 3 g protein

sure to "peas" dinners

curry in a hurry

Makes 4 servings

I'M BY NO MEANS AN INDIAN FOOD EXPERT. I'D NEVER even had Indian food until I had graduated from law school, passed the Bar and was working as an associate at a small law firm. I was the only female attorney at the firm. Try as I might, I couldn't hide my femininity. I wore pink suits with matching lipstick and I kept a Tinker Bell figurine on my desk. Clearly, I commanded respect. For the most part, though, I could go about my work and let my pleadings and memorandums speak for themselves, without any degree of judgment on my appearance or gender. That is, until we had our weekly meetings.

Every Monday "the boys" would decide what we'd order for lunch, and nine times out of ten, it was Indian food. I always planned ahead, bringing my own modest lunch, quietly eating a cup of soup and a clump of grapes in the most inconspicuous manner possible. If I could seamlessly detract attention from what I was or wasn't eating, maybe I could still be "one of the guys." I'd thought the fruit inclusion out carefully. An apple was far too crunchy. An orange's fragrance commands a room and since I'd have to peel it, I'd end up with a large pile of rind on the table. I might as well have screamed, "Look at my huge uterus!" while I was at it. And a banana? Completely out of the question.

After about two weeks of observing the opening of grease-soaked takeout boxes and huge slabs of oily bread being dabbed in pungent, brightly colored sauces, the senior partner insisted I try a plate. Can't I just eat a banana in a bikini instead? I was pleasantly surprised though at the familiar tastes: curry, coconut milk, ginger, garlic, cilantro, lime. And though I still brought my lunches to those weekly meetings, I was open to the idea of enjoying Indian cuisine, at least until I got pregnant and blending in with the boys wasn't even fathomable.

I can't say that I miss the practice of law, especially in an environment where I felt uncomfortable in my own girly skin. I'm in a place now where high heels are encouraged, feather boas are smiled upon and being a princess is the norm. I'm no longer deposing witnesses, though I do spend a lot of time in mediation, usually settling not for hundreds of thousands of dollars, but an extra bedtime story. However, I've created an at-home curry that takes me back to that tiny law library every time I smell it bubbling away on the stove. There are no spices to grind and it comes together in a hurry. Every member of our family is happy to come to the table to enjoy this dish, even the little ladies.

INGREDIENTS

Marinade:

¼ cup lime juice

1 tablespoon reduced-sodium soy sauce

2 tablespoons agave nectar or honey

2 tablespoons warm water

Curry:

1 16-ounce package extra-firm tofu, drained and pressed using technique on p. xxix, and cut into 10 2 × 3-inch slabs

1 teaspoon minced garlic

1 tablespoon minced ginger

1 cup asparagus spears, trimmed and cut into 2-inch pieces

1 cup carrots, peeled and cut into coins

1 cup broccoli florets

1 cup cauliflower florets

1 cup red bell pepper, cut into 1½-inch pieces

1½ tablespoons curry powder

1 14-ounce can light coconut milk

1 tablespoon arrowroot

1 lime, divided in half

2 tablespoons fresh basil

2 tablespoons fresh cilantro, chopped

organic sugar or stevia to taste

2 cups cooked brown rice

Garnish:

roasted cashews, chopped cilantro and remaining lime cut into wedges

DIRECTIONS

1 Combine all marinade ingredients in a pie plate or a shallow baking dish. Place pressed tofu in marinade for at least 30 minutes.

2 Preheat the broiler and spray a cookie sheet with cooking spray.

3 Spray a large skillet or wok with cooking spray and place over medium-high heat. Sauté garlic, ginger, asparagus, carrots, broccoli, cauliflower and peppers for 4 to 7 minutes. Remove from pan and place in a large bowl covered with tinfoil to keep vegetables warm.

4 In the meantime, place tofu on prepared cookie sheet and broil for 6 minutes on each side.

5 In the same skillet, heat curry powder over medium heat until aromatic. Add coconut milk and bring to a low boil.

6 Remove approximately 2 tablespoons of the curry milk mixture and place in a small dish. Whisk arrowroot into dish until all lumps are gone, and then add mixture back into the sauce. Simmer until thickened.

7 Add vegetables back into pan and add juice from half of the lime and chopped herbs. Sweeten as desired.

8 Heat thoroughly and serve over brown rice. Pass cashews, chopped cilantro and remaining lime cut into wedges at the table for garnish.

NUTRITION INFORMATION PER SERVING: 431 calories, 17 g total fat, 7 g saturated fat, 0 mg cholesterol, 180 mg sodium, 46 g carbohydrates, 7 g fiber, 24 g protein

pea POINTS

You may be surprised at how much little taste buds can enjoy curry. Adjust the amounts to your liking and remember that early exposure to exotic foods can set your little Peas up for a lifetime of eating adventures.

sure to "peas" dinners

indian shepherd's pie (page 176)

indian shepherd's pie

Makes 4 large servings

ONE OF THE BEST THINGS ABOUT HOLIDAY DINNERS, IN MY FRUGAL YET creative mind, is finding ingenious ways to use the leftovers. Even though I'm not making turkey sandwiches with dried out, overcooked birds anymore, I still like to turn our leftovers into Comfort Food: Part Two. This shepherd's pie came about when I had abundant sweet potatoes, roasted chickpeas and quinoa after our first vegetarian Thanksgiving (admittedly, not everyone in our extended family was on board, including our retired butcher patriarch, Papa). Ironically, this dish is now a star in its own right. And I'm proud to say, this shepherd's pie is 100 percent sheep-free.

INGREDIENTS

1 pound sweet potatoes, peeled and cubed in 1-inch cubes

1 pound butternut squash, peeled and cubed in 1-inch cubes

1 tablespoon vegan margarine (i.e., Earth Balance)

2 tablespoons non-dairy or organic milk

½ teaspoon cinnamon

1⅓ cups water

⅔ cup dry quinoa, rinsed and drained

1 cup chopped onion

1 cup chopped carrots

1 cup canned chickpeas, drained and rinsed

2 cloves garlic, minced

6 vegetarian sausage links (i.e., Morningstar), cooked according to package directions and cut into bite-sized chunks

1 cup vegetable broth

1 tablespoon curry powder

2 teaspoons coriander

½ teaspoon salt

organic sugar to taste (optional)

1 cup organic spinach, chopped

½ cup dried cranberries

DIRECTIONS

1 Preheat oven to 400 degrees.

2 Bring a large pot of water to a boil and add sweet potatoes and butternut squash. Cover, reduce heat and simmer for about 20 minutes.

3 When potatoes and squash are fork tender, drain and add to a large bowl. Using an electric or stand mixer, add margarine, milk and cinnamon and whip until smooth and fluffy.

4 Meanwhile, in a smaller pot, bring 1⅓ cups of water to a boil and add rinsed quinoa. Cover, reduce heat and simmer for about 10 minutes.

5 In a large skillet sprayed with cooking spray, sauté onion, carrots and chickpeas until vegetables are tender, about 6 minutes. Add garlic and briefly sauté for a minute. Add sausage, broth, curry, coriander and salt and allow to simmer.

6 When quinoa is ready, add to pan and cook for an additional 2 to 3 minutes to allow the sauce to thicken and the grain to absorb some of the sauce.

7 Sweeten sauce to taste with organic sugar, if desired. Toss in chopped spinach and dried cranberries and stir until combined.

8 Spray a 2-quart casserole dish with cooking spray and add quinoa vegetable mixture to the dish. Top with the mashed squash and sweet potatoes and spread to evenly cover the filling.

9 Bake uncovered for 25 to 30 minutes.

NUTRITION INFORMATION PER SERVING: 357 calories, 11 g total fat, 2 g saturated fat, 0 mg cholesterol, 874 mg sodium, 75 g carbohydrates, 12 g fiber, 18 g protein

pea POINTS

Experiment with any leftover vegetable combinations you may have on hand. Leftover Pumpkin Spice–Roasted Chickpeas (p. 105) are especially fantastic in this recipe.

sure to "peas" dinners

vegetarian pad thai

Makes 4 large servings

WE DIDN'T EAT OUT MUCH WHEN I WAS A KID, BUT IF WE DID, WE WENT to the local Coco's where we cozied up in a pleather booth, circled HOT DOG in a placemat word search with stubby, overused crayons and drank room-temperature milk out of amber-colored glasses. There was nothing exotic about their food, but you knew what you were getting, and if you were under twelve and accompanied by an adult, you were getting it for 99¢. So when a friend invited me out for Thai food when I was in college, I was nervous. I frantically scanned the menu for the few American items that would undoubtedly be offered on the kids' menu. After realizing this wasn't an option, I turned back to the grown-up offerings. Rather than try to pronounce a dish that I had no idea how to say, much less what it contained, after my friend ordered I pulled the

old, "Mmm, that sounds good. I'll have that." Lucky for me, "that" turned out to be pad thai, and I was instantly smitten. My at-home re-creation may be slightly Americanized, but at least we have quality crayons.

INGREDIENTS

Marinade:

3 tablespoons hoisin sauce

¼ cup reduced-sodium soy sauce

⅓ cup organic ketchup

⅓ cup fresh lime juice

⅓ cup warm water

3 tablespoons organic sugar

Pad Thai:

1 16-ounce package extra-firm tofu, drained and pressed using technique on p. xxix, and cut into 10 2 × 3-inch slabs

6 ounces rice noodles

2 cups asparagus spears, trimmed and cut into 2-inch pieces

1 cup carrots, peeled and cut into coins

2 cups broccoli florets

1 6-ounce can bamboo shoots, drained

Garnish:
lime wedges, cilantro, mint and peanuts

pea POINTS

I use this marinade for broiled tofu even if I'm not making the pad thai. The slightly sweet and tangy tofu is fantastic on a salad or in a wrap, and the girls love it straight-up, as long as "straight-up" means with a side of organic ketchup for dipping.

DIRECTIONS

1 Combine all marinade ingredients in a pie plate or a shallow baking dish. Place pressed tofu in marinade for at least 30 minutes.

2 Preheat the broiler and spray a cookie sheet with cooking spray.

3 Reserving marinade, place tofu on prepared cookie sheet and broil for 6 minutes on each side. Cut cooked tofu into cubes and set aside.

4 Meanwhile, prepare rice noodles according to package directions. Drain noodles, run under cold water and set aside.

5 Spray a large skillet or wok with cooking spray and place over medium-high heat. Sauté asparagus, carrots, broccoli and bamboo for 4 to 7 minutes. Remove from pan and place in a large bowl covered with tinfoil to keep vegetables warm.

6 In the same skillet, heat the remaining marinade and add rice noodles. Add vegetables back into pan and add tofu. Heat thoroughly.

7 Pass lime wedges, chopped cilantro, chopped mint and peanuts at the table for garnish.

NUTRITION INFORMATION PER SERVING: 451 calories, 11 g total fat, 2 g saturated fat, 0 mg cholesterol, 881 mg sodium, 70 g carbohydrates, 8 g fiber, 25 g protein

sure to "peas" dinners

lulu's mac and cheese

Makes 6 to 8 servings

THERE ARE TWO KINDS OF MAC AND CHEESE IN THIS WORLD: THE KIND that comes in the box and the kind that I wish tasted more like the kind that came in the box. I know what you are thinking. I must not have had very good homemade mac and cheese. On the contrary, my grammy was such a famed macaroni and cheese maker that every year for my dad's birthday she would give him a big, white Corning Ware dish of the stuff. I swear that casserole dish weighed twelve pounds, due primarily to the fact that she used an entire two-pound loaf of sharp cheddar cheese in her mac. There's something about that much cheese, though, it just doesn't melt like the oozy sauce in the foil packet. I didn't mess around with the powder. I was a Deluxe girl myself.

The cheese was the least of my problems with Grammy's mac, though. In addition to the two pounds of cheese, she used about eight cloves of garlic and an entire onion in her recipe. I actually dreaded opening the refrigerator for the week of my dad's birthday, because as soon as I cracked the seal on the door and the little light came on, my nostrils would be assaulted with the overwhelming stench of garlic and onions. My dad would come home for lunch and as soon as I heard his car pull in the driveway, I'd run and hide. I'd hear the clang of the casserole dish lid, as he scooped out a congealed blob on his plate. The buttons on the microwave would beep as he entered the time and then it'd whir as it spun around the pungent pasta, heating it just enough to send the stench down the hallway to my room. He'd lower himself into the recliner, switch on *General Hospital* and eat his smelly lunch. The odor was so strong, I believed that if I opened my door, I might actually be able to see the cartoonish, wavy lines of stank traveling through the air. Yet one more smelly push for me back to the faithful blue box.

That's not to say that it isn't possible to have a bad batch of mac and cheese from a box. By far the worst mac and cheese I've ever had came from a package and was so offensive, I think Pea Daddy, the girls, my dentist and many a door-to-door solicitor are familiar with this story.

When I was in fifth grade, a new girl moved in down the street. She was from California, highlighted hair, eye makeup and, at the pinnacle of my fascination, two different neon-colored slouchy socks. Totally. I tried to make fast friends with Missy (*not* Melissa), a feat that was made easier by her obvious interest in my older brother.

It was a wintry day that January when I met the worst mac and cheese of my life. The streets were covered with at least a foot and a half of snow and, much to my delight, Missy and I were thrown together by geographic proximity. She didn't have a whole lot of other playmates to choose from at that moment. We spent the day playing in the snow, her perm looking awesome in the misty flakes, my own hair looking like the crazy cat lady's who lived down the block and yelled at the mailbox. We sledded down the hill and built a snowman, or at least I did while Missy and my brother chased each other with snowballs. It came time for lunch and Missy's mom invited us in for hot cocoa and, you guessed it, mac and cheese.

We kicked off our boots, snow pants and jackets and raced up to the kitchen, eagerly waiting for her mom to turn away from the stove and place a steamy bowl in front of us. Nothing could have prepared me for what laid before me. As soon as I spied the bowl, I knew something was wrong. The macaroni was floating in the "cheese." I use the word *cheese* lightly, since this was not cheese sauce that a heavy hand with the milk could explain. It was far too watery, far too thin and far too orange. Even without the experience of Home Economics under my belt (that would come several awkward adolescent years later), I immediately knew what had happened. Missy's mom had not drained the cooking water from the pasta before adding the envelope of cheese powder. Who does that?! Apparently the type of woman that lets her ten-year-old wear eyeliner and mismatched socks. Apparently Missy's mom.

peas and thank you

Stranger still, Missy dug into that orange brothy dish like it was her last meal. I was at a loss as to what to do. I was starving. I couldn't offend Missy's mom, and I couldn't offend Missy, not if I wanted her to flirt with my brother and pretend to be my friend any longer. So I went fishing. I scooped out as many waterlogged macaroni as I could and gummed them down until I could run home and find something that even a chimpanzee could have properly prepared. At that point, I would have traded all of my Jordan Knight–covered *Bop* magazines for even Grammy's mac and cheese.

In a surprising twist, years later, I have a child who would eat mac and cheese for breakfast, lunch, dinner and communion, if given the opportunity. Since I'm not crazy about giving my girls much of anything that comes in a box, I had no choice but to come up with a homemade version. Even more surprisingly, I'm actually crazy about this recipe. The key to its deliciousness is a quality vegan or organic cheese. And if you drain the noodles properly, I promise, it doesn't stink.

pea POINTS

This recipe loves a great add-in, like crumbled tempeh bacon, veggie pepperoni slices or, if you are willing, even green veggies. No surprise, but we find *peas* especially delicious.

INGREDIENTS

½ pound elbow macaroni (preferably whole wheat)

2 tablespoons vegan margarine (i.e., Earth Balance)

½ block silken tofu

2 tablespoons non-dairy or organic milk (unflavored/unsweetened)

1 teaspoon salt

fresh black pepper

½ teaspoon dry mustard

8 ounces non-dairy (i.e., Daiya cheddar shreds) or organic cheddar, shredded

DIRECTIONS

1   Bring a large pot of salted water to a boil. Add the macaroni and cook according to package directions. Drain well.

2   Return to the pot and melt in the margarine. Toss to coat.

3   Blend together the tofu, milk, salt, pepper and mustard in a blender or food processor.

4   Stir into the pasta and add the cheese. Over low heat, continue to stir for 3 minutes or until creamy.

NUTRITION INFORMATION PER SERVING (for 8 servings): 198 calories, 7 g total fat, 3 g saturated fat, 15 mg cholesterol, 760 mg sodium, 26 g carbohydrates, 3 g fiber, 9 g protein

183

sure to "peas" dinners

pea daddy's jambalaya (page 186)

pea daddy's jambalaya

Makes 4 daddy-sized servings

AFTER A FEW DAYS, WEEKS, MONTHS OR YEARS OF MARRIAGE, EVERY wife finds that her husband has characteristics that, while once endearing, are enough to make her want to drag her man on to a national television show in front of a panel of B-list celebrities for judgment. You don't win money. You don't win a car. You don't even get to fly to L.A. for taping—you get to appear via satellite in your own home so that America can see you in your element, airing your dirty laundry amid piles of your dirty laundry. What prize could possibly be worth this potential humiliation? The simple yet glorious honor of being declared *right* by someone other than yourself.

The issue in our household for several years has been Pea Daddy's knack for holding on to things. While my motto is, "When in doubt, throw it out," Pea Daddy's catchphrase is, "I could use that someday." His penchant for pre-serving possessions hasn't gotten completely out of hand. Unlike an extreme hoarder's home, our home has a visable living room floor and I haven't put out an APB on a missing cat. Although, should Pea Kitty disappear, my bulletin would more likely be, "Free at last, free at last!" Pea Daddy's talent lies more in refusing to get rid of things that have had a good life, fulfilled their purpose on this earth and are ready to follow the white light and move on to a better place, like Goodwill.

The absolute worst offender of the "I've Got a Few Good Years Left in Me" Club is, without a doubt, Pea Daddy's bed pillow. I understand that everyone has his or her favorite pillow. There is something magical about finding just the right pillow with the right firmness, the right height, the right give, the right fluff. However, there is something creepy about using a pillow that was your great-grandfather's, a pillow that is brown from God knows what bodily secretions that again, may not even be yours, but could quite possibly be your great-grandfather's. I knew it was a problem when I grabbed a hazmat suit, polypropylene gloves and kitchen tongs and inspected the barely attached tag. I gasped when I read, PATENT PENDING: 1946.

My pleas, threats and bribes went unacknowledged until one day, Pea Daddy became tangled in a web of his own idiosyncrasies. Then came the most memorable text message I have ever received, five beautiful words that made me want to turn a cartwheel on the one strip of carpet in our bedroom not covered in baseball cards, old newspapers clippings and bedding of the elderly. My girlfriend Kalin, knowing of both Pea Daddy's pillow attachment and his attachment of an entirely different kind texted simply, "Tommy Bahama pillows @ Costco."

I knew I had to handle the situation with care. I couldn't force the dirty, dead pillow from Pea Daddy's hands, but simply needed to make him consider where his loyalties, and his head should lie. Sure, he and Great-Gramps had shared head sweat, dust mites and skin cells for years, but Pea Daddy wouldn't turn anything down that smelled slightly of coconut oil, was embroidered with a palm tree and was overpriced, just like the Islands. As we went to Costco later that day, I nonchalantly waved my hand over at the alluring marshmallows of cleanliness, and said, "Hmm. Tommy Bahama pillows. Interesting." As Pea Daddy plucked the fluffy, pure pillows from the shelf, I tried not to squeal with delight. I'd broken him.

It's easy, after a good night's sleep on clean pillows, to look at Pea Daddy's attachment issues and realize how endearing they might be. He knows what he loves, and he loves it with every fiber of his being until every fiber of *its* being can't take it anymore. Beyond risks of public nudity and bubonic plague from ancestral housewares, Pea Daddy has this same undying devotion to his favorite musicians, his favorite movies and his favorite foods, meaning I had to come up with an impressive meat-free jambalaya if this whole "vegetarian thing" was going to stick.

I'm happy to report that Pea Daddy's still a vegetarian, and now has a favorite meal, and thankfully a wife, that he is forever devoted to. Sometimes that's even better than being right.

pea POINTS

Pea Daddy loves this jambalaya with a batch of Cowgirl Cornbread (p. 101) on the side. To make this meal even easier, use precooked brown rice that can be found in the grains aisle or the frozen food section of your grocer.

sure to "peas" dinners

INGREDIENTS

4 meatless sausages (i.e., Tofurky or field roast), sliced

1 cup red bell pepper, chopped

1 cup onion, chopped

1 cup celery (approximately 2 stalks), chopped

2 teaspoons minced garlic

1 teaspoon dried basil

1 teaspoon dried oregano

1 teaspoon dried parsley

1 15-ounce can organic fire-roasted tomatoes

1 cup vegetable broth

3 cups cooked brown rice or quinoa

salt and pepper to taste

DIRECTIONS

1 Spray a large skillet with cooking spray and place over medium-high heat.

2 Add sausages and cook until beginning to brown, approximately 5 minutes.

3 Add peppers, onions and celery and cook until vegetables are crisp tender, about 7 minutes.

4 Add garlic, basil, oregano and parsley and sauté for an additional minute. Add tomatoes and broth and bring to a low boil, then lower heat. Cover and simmer for 10 minutes.

5 Add cooked rice or quinoa and allow to absorb sauce and flavors, stirring and cooking for an additional 5 to 10 minutes. Season with salt and pepper to taste.

NUTRITION INFORMATION PER SERVING: 281 calories, 6 g total fat, 1 g saturated fat, 0 mg cholesterol, 389 mg sodium, 49 g carbohydrates, 6 g fiber, 10 g protein

peas and thank you

mama thai's cashew pineapple stir-fry

Makes 4 servings

THERE'S NO TYPO THERE, MY FRIENDS. THIS RECIPE IS NAMED FOR A whole different "Mama," and you guessed it, that Mama is Thai. When Pea Daddy agreed to go meat-free, I had a strategy, a strategy based in nostalgia, trickery and flat-out flavor thievery. First stop: Mama Thai.

When Pea Daddy and I were first-year associates, one of our biggest worries, aside from how to turn emailing each other and conducting "intensive research" on Facebook into 7.5 billable hours each day, was where we would eat lunch. Our offices were only half a mile apart, and unless I had a lunch meeting where I was forced to eat a cup of soup while my colleagues dipped greasy roti into stanky curries, Pea Daddy always came and took me out to eat. It was the best hour of my day. He'd pull up in his old Acura sedan, the one whose antenna groaned at the idea of having to actually exert itself and pick up some reception, and my senior partner would make some crack about some dude in a sweater-vest waiting for me in my town car.

Inevitably, we'd end up at Mama Thai's. The true name of the establishment was Thailand Restaurant, but everyone called it Mama Thai's because of the woman behind the beaded curtain. Her name was Mo, and she was as sweet as Thai iced tea. Every day I'd place my order of Thai Basil Stir-Fry, no rice, minus the mushrooms, plus extra basil, and every day she'd tell me, "You need to eat more!" Her husband was the cook, and he'd peek out from his kitchen window while he was picking out my mushrooms. He'd grin and waive vigorously, and since he didn't speak English, Mo would translate his motions to mean that I was his "favorite customer." I'd like to believe that it had something to do with a basil surplus that I was helping to diminish, but I fear it had more to do with the Ally McBeal suit I was sporting.

Pea Daddy's daily order was the Thai Cashew Pineapple Stir-Fry, a delicious combination of crisp celery, sweet pineapple and rich cashews over rice. After a few weeks, we never had to even place our orders, we'd just walk in, Mo would nod and a few minutes later I'd have my Thai Basil Stir-Fry and Pea Daddy would have his cashews. That is until nine months before Gigi's birth.

Suddenly, rice seemed like a fabulous idea and stir-fries turned into curries. As I started putting on the seventy pounds I would gain over the course of the pregnancy, Mama Thai was overjoyed. "Ahhh…that much better!" she would say, approvingly. Not only would I sop up every last grain of rice with the thick, rich yellow sauce, I'd dig into Pea Daddy's leftovers, too. And with every order, every bite, and every miniskirted power suit outgrown, my kitchen friend would wave just as excitedly when we'd walk in the door. True love isn't conditional.

Sadly, the Thailand Restaurant closed soon after Gigi was born. Mo and her husband wanted to move closer to their family in Florida, and though we miss their food, it seemed fitting since we, too, were opening a new chapter in our lives. I no longer have lunch dates with Pea Daddy in his first car. I no longer fudge billable hours to impress condescending partners. And as I grow older and tote two young girls into restaurants with me, I no longer have chefs waving to me from the kitchen. But Pea Daddy still gets Thai Cashew Pineapple Stir-Fry, though I've swapped his chicken for tofu. Like I said, true love isn't conditional.

INGREDIENTS

2 tablespoons lemon juice

1 tablespoon water

2 teaspoons organic sugar

1 16-ounce package organic tofu, drained and pressed using technique on p. xxix, and cut into 10 2 × 3-inch slabs

1 bell pepper (orange, yellow or red), seeded and chopped

2 stalks celery, chopped

1 cup carrots, peeled and chopped

1 20-ounce can pineapple chunks in juice

2 tablespoons cornstarch

¼ cup reduced-sodium soy sauce

¼ cup apple cider vinegar

1 6-ounce can sliced water chestnuts

2 cups steamed brown rice

½ cup cashews

pea POINTS

You can make this dish into a restaurant style sweet-and-sour by using meat-free nuggets in place of the tofu. MSG and fortune cookies not included.

DIRECTIONS

1 In a shallow dish or pie plate, combine lemon juice, water and sugar. Marinate tofu for 30 minutes or overnight.

2 Preheat oven to 425 degrees.

3 Bake marinated tofu for 6 to 7 minutes on each side. Set aside to cool, and then cut into bite-sized pieces.

4 In a large skillet coated with cooking spray, sauté peppers, celery and carrots over medium-high heat until crisp tender, about 5 minutes.

5 Drain pineapple, reserving juice, and set chunks aside. Add cornstarch, soy sauce and vinegar to juice and whisk until smooth.

6 Add sauce to cooked vegetables and bring to a gentle boil until thickened, about 1 minute. Once sauce has thickened, add pineapple, water chestnuts and baked tofu and heat through.

7 Serve over brown rice and top with cashews.

NUTRITION INFORMATION PER SERVING: 410 calories, 16 g total fat, 3 g saturated fat, 0 mg cholesterol, 596 mg sodium, 64 g carbohydrates, 10 g fiber, 26 g protein

falafel with tzatziki sauce

Makes 24 to 32 falafel and approximately 1½ cups sauce

I HAPPEN TO BE MULTILINGUAL. I SPEAK ENGLISH RELATIVELY WELL.
I studied Spanish for six years. For some reason I still don't entirely understand myself, I subjected myself to the task of learning the very dead language Latin. *Veni, vidi, vici.* My greatest language accomplishment, though? I speak Lulu. And now you can, too.

Here is volume one of your Wiki-PEA-dia guide to the language of Lulu:

Frownies: *noun; a baked, dense chewy cake, usually made with chocolate; as in, "Mommy, I dropped* frownies *in your purse!"*

Hanitizer: *noun; an antiseptic solution used as an alternative to washing hands with soap and water; as in, "It's okay, I washed your purse with* hanitizer!"

Tummus: *noun; 1) a popular fictional locomotive; 2) a delicious Mediterranean chickpea spread; as in, "My mommy makes the best* tummus *ever…see page 116!"*

Hoopa loop: *verb; to make a plastic hoop rotate around the body by swinging one's hips; as in, "I'm trying to* hoopa loop!"

Crummery: *adj.; in an untidy condition; as in, "This peanut butter makes my hands all* crummery!"

Keenie: *noun; a two-piece bathing suit for women or girls; as in, "Mommy, I tinkled in my* keenie!"

Falawesome: *noun; a small croquette made with ground chickpeas and spices; as in "More* falawesome, *please!"*

sure to "peas" dinners

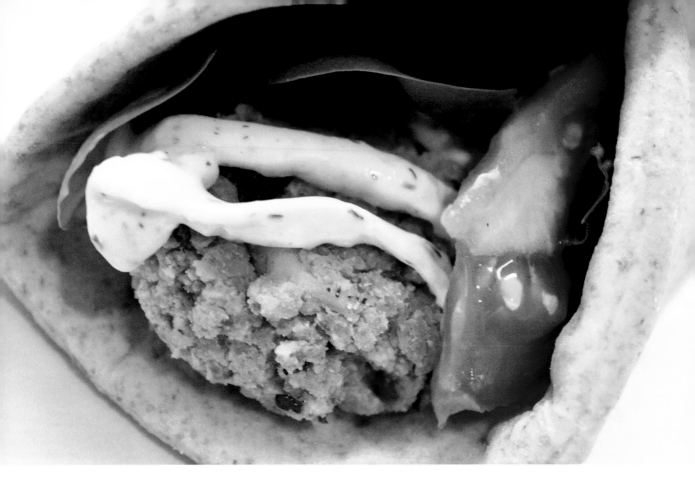

INGREDIENTS

Falafel:

8 ounces firm or extra-firm tofu, drained and pressed using technique on p. xxix

1 14.5-ounce can chickpeas, drained and rinsed

1½ tablespoons minced garlic

2 tablespoons tahini

2 tablespoons lemon juice

1 cup old-fashioned oats, finely ground

2 teaspoons cumin

2 tablespoons nutritional yeast

1 to 2 tablespoons water, if necessary

⅓ cup cilantro, chopped

⅓ cup mint leaves, chopped

salt and pepper to taste

Tzatziki Sauce:

1 cup silken tofu (firm or extra firm)

2 tablespoons vegan mayonnaise
(i.e., Vegenaise)

2 teaspoons minced garlic

2 tablespoons lemon juice

½ teaspoon salt

2 teaspoons dried dill

1 small cucumber, peeled, seeded
and chopped

DIRECTIONS

1 Preheat oven to 350 degrees.

2 For falafel, in a food processor or blender, combine tofu, chickpeas,
   garlic, tahini and lemon juice until smooth. Set aside.

3 In a large bowl, combine oats, cumin and nutritional yeast.

4 Add chickpea mixture to dry mixture and stir until combined.
   You may add a tablespoon or two of water if the mixture seems too dry.
   Fold in chopped herbs and season with salt and pepper as desired.

5 Form falafel into 24 to 32 golf-ball-sized balls and place on a baking
   sheet that has been sprayed with cooking spray. Bake for 20 minutes,
   flipping falafel once after 10 minutes.

6 For tzatziki, combine tofu, mayonnaise, garlic, lemon juice, salt and
   dill in a blender or food processor until smooth. Fold in cucumber
   and chill until serving.

7 Serve falafel warm with tzatziki sauce.

NUTRITION INFORMATION PER FALAFEL (for 32 falafel): 40 calories, 1 g total fat,
0 g saturated fat, 0 mg cholesterol, 54 mg sodium, 6 g carbohydrates, 1 g fiber, 3 g protein

pea POINTS

Stuff the falafel
into whole
wheat pitas with
tomato, lettuce
and tzatziki for a
traditional falafel
sandwich. Serve
with raw veg-
etables and Crazy
Good tummus, er
Hummus (p. 116)
on the side for
a falawesome
Greek meal.

sure to "peas" dinners

Sweet Endings for Sweet Peas 5

ONE OF MY MOTHER'S FAVORITE PHRASES—RIGHT UP THERE WITH "Because I said so," and "If you get any closer to the ledge, I'm going to have a heart attack"—is "You don't need dessert *every* night!" In theory, she's probably right, though she really does need an intervention to overcome her unreasonable fear of heights. Still, I can't help but believe that we all *do* need a special treat every night.

As a parent, I've come to appreciate the importance of rituals in a child's life. Sometimes these rituals are treated like you are pulling out tiny toddler fingernails with rusty metal pliers, like the daily task of taming Gigi's unfortunate morning bedhead/Diana Ross impression, while others are not only beloved, but expected, like the fact that every time an oven mitt gets pulled

out of the kitchen drawer it will inevitably act as a claw and pinch any child within a three-foot radius. The beauty of childhood rituals is that in a life of serial unexpected events, there is always something that the girls can count on for familiarity and comfort.

No matter what, every morning I'm going to terrorize Gigi with a comb and a squirt bottle between her getting dressed and brushing her teeth, every time that oven door slams shut, Lulu's going to look around for a pot holder claw, and every night between dinner and bath time, someone between the ages of two and thirty-two is going to ask, "Can I have a treat?" Armed with the recipes here, I'll grab the cookie jar or open the fridge and offer something that is special enough to be considered "dessert," yet nutritious enough to eat anytime. Some nights it's as simple as fresh berries, and often it's one of the recipes in this chapter.

I've found a way to make my family's favorite desserts, while giving them treats that are nutritious and healthy enough to celebrate *every* day with. Now that's a ritual I can get behind.

double chocolate/single chin brownies

Makes 1 8 × 8-inch pan

SOME OF THE BEST THINGS IN LIFE ARE THE MOST SIMPLE: SIX-FEET-WIDE kiddie swimming pools shaped like turtles, a hug from Lulu when she's *not* sopping wet from Mr. Turtle and a batch of brownies with nine ingredients, virtually no fat and a less-than-thirty-minute prep time. Just don't go eating these brownies in the pool. Explaining the residual floaters…not so simple.

INGREDIENTS

¾ cup whole wheat pastry or white whole wheat flour

⅓ cup cocoa powder

2 teaspoons baking powder

½ teaspoon baking soda

½ teaspoon salt

1 cup unsweetened applesauce

½ cup organic sugar

1 teaspoon vanilla

½ cup dark chocolate chips

DIRECTIONS

1   Preheat oven to 350 degrees.

2   In a large bowl, combine flour, cocoa, baking powder, baking soda and salt.

3   In a smaller bowl, combine applesauce, sugar and vanilla.

4   Add wet mixture to dry ingredients and stir until just combined. Fold in chocolate chips.

5   Pour batter into an 8 × 8-inch pan that has been sprayed with cooking spray. Bake for 18 to 20 minutes, or until brownies are set and edges are starting to pull away from the pan. Let cool before cutting.

NUTRITION INFORMATION PER SERVING: (for 8 servings) 143 calories, 4 g total fat, 2 g saturated fat, 0 mg cholesterol, 122 mg sodium, 26 g carbohydrates, 2 g fiber, 2 g protein

anytime cookies

Makes 12 large cookies

I HAVE AN INCREDIBLE BABYSITTER. EVERY DAY, THIS BABYSITTER BUYS me an hour to clean the maple syrup off the placemats, un-embed the raisins from the carpet or, on the days when hygiene is actually a priority, wash my hair in the kitchen sink. I can't leave a two- and four-year-old unattended while I reenact an Herbal Essences commercial in my shower. Believe me, I've tried, and thanks to a biting incident between "Repeat" and "Rinse," I wound up sporting conditioner in my hair for the rest of the day, leaving it even greasier than before.

So while I'm sudsing in the kitchen, I leave my kids in the very responsible care of this fantastic caregiver: first name, *Sesame*; last name, *Street*. Before you judge me and cite all sorts of studies by the American Pediatric Society, I'd like to note that my daughter asked me tonight if Brussels sprouts were from Belgium. I wish I'd taught her that, but geography was never my strong suit. I think it's safe to assume this tidbit was a result of educational programming.

I grew up watching *Sesame Street*, and in spite of my lack of knowledge of European cities and their vegetable offspring, I turned out reasonably well. However, imagine my surprise one morning when I heard Cookie Monster serenading my children with a song about how cookies are a "sometimes" food. I gasped. I fell to my knees. I felt much like I did when I found out George Michael was gay. Here I thought he "wanted *my* sex." Guess not.

While I, of all people, can appreciate the attempt of my babysitter to educate my children on healthy foods and "sometimes" treats, I was resentful that Cookie Monster was being robbed of his identity. I felt motivated to take action. With a spatula in hand and a dream in my heart, I created this cookie that's just so darn deliciously healthy, it can be enjoyed ANYTIME.

Cookie Monster, this one's for you.

INGREDIENTS

4 tablespoons ground flaxseed, divided

½ cup water

1 cup unbleached organic flour

½ cup organic whole wheat pastry or white whole wheat flour

½ cup old-fashioned oats

½ teaspoon baking soda

½ teaspoon ground cinnamon

¼ teaspoon ground nutmeg

¼ cup unrefined organic sugar

¼ cup unrefined organic brown sugar

¼ cup canola oil

¼ cup non-dairy or organic milk

1 teaspoon vanilla extract

¼ cup roughly chopped dried apricots

¼ cup raisins

¼ cup chopped almonds (or any other nut desired) and/or dark chocolate chips

pea POINTS

I make a batch of these to take with us when traveling. They can stand in for any meal in a pinch, aren't too messy to eat in the car and make air travel companions jealous when those little bags of pretzels are passed out.

DIRECTIONS

1   Preheat oven to 350 degrees.

2   In a small bowl, combine 2 tablespoons ground flaxseed with ½ cup water. Set aside.

3   In a large bowl, combine flours, oats, baking soda, remaining 2 tablespoons ground flaxseed and spices.

4   To flaxseed-water mixture, add sugars, oil, milk, vanilla, apricots and raisins.

5   Add wet mixture to dry ingredients, stirring until just combined. Fold in nuts and/or chocolate chips.

6   Drop 12 spoonfuls of cookie dough onto a cookie sheet sprayed lightly with cooking spray. The dough will not spread much during baking, so press dough into a flat, cookielike shape.

7   Bake for 12 minutes. Cool for 1 minute on cookie sheet and then transfer to a cooling rack. Let cookies cool completely before moving them to an airtight container.

NUTRITION INFORMATION PER SERVING: 186 calories, 8 g total fat, 1 g saturated fat, 0 mg cholesterol, 8 mg sodium, 28 g carbohydrates, 4 g fiber, 4 g protein

peas and thank you

cutout sugar cookies

Makes 24 to 32 cookies

MY SUGAR COOKIES HAVE ALWAYS BEEN FAMOUSLY GOOD, AT THE office, at holiday parties, even given away as favors at our wedding. You can imagine that packing 250 sugar cookies into cellophane bags was exactly what I wanted to be doing three days before walking down the aisle. They were so soft, sweet and buttery that whenever I served these cookies, at least one partygoer would inevitably ask for the recipe, and inevitably, I'd lie. "It's a secret family recipe," I'd shyly reply. Here's the secret: I adopted Betty Crocker. That's right, I'd buy the little red pouch, add an egg and do exactly what it takes to make dreamy cookies. I'd underbake them. Since cleaning up our diets, one of my most lofty goals was to create a dairy-free sugar cookie that was every bit as amazing as my dirty little secret. Mission accomplished. I'd like to look you straight in the eye and give you the recipe.

INGREDIENTS

2 ½ cups unbleached organic flour

2 teaspoons baking powder

½ teaspoon salt

1 cup organic sugar

¼ cup non-dairy or organic milk

2 teaspoons vanilla extract

1 cup vegan margarine
(i.e., Earth Balance)

Icing:
¾ cup vegan margarine
(i.e., Earth Balance)

½ teaspoon vanilla extract

dash of salt

2 cups organic powdered sugar

1 to 2 tablespoons non-dairy or organic milk, as needed

Optional:
natural food coloring, sprinkles, et cetera

DIRECTIONS

1 In a small bowl, combine flour, baking powder and salt.

2 In the bowl of a stand mixer or a large mixing bowl, beat together sugar, milk, vanilla and margarine. Gradually add dry ingredients to the large bowl, mixing until a dough comes together.

3 Remove dough from bowl and wrap in plastic wrap. Refrigerate for 1 to 3 hours, or until dough is chilled and firm.

4 Preheat oven to 350 degrees.

5 Remove dough from fridge and roll out onto a floured board with a floured rolling pin until dough is about ¾-inch thick. Using cookie cutters, cut into desired shapes and carefully transfer to a cookie sheet.

6 Bake for 10 to 12 minutes, until edges are slightly starting to brown. Do not overbake. Allow cookies to cool on cookie sheet for 1 minute before transferring them to a cooling rack.

7 For icing, beat together all ingredients except milk then slowly add in milk until you've reached desired consistency. Mix in food coloring, if using. Cookies should be completely cooled before icing. Garnish with sprinkles, if using.

NUTRITION INFORMATION PER SERVING (for 32 cookies): 121 calories, 3 g total fat, 1 g saturated fat, 0 mg cholesterol, 90 mg sodium, 22 g carbohydrates, 0 g fiber, 1 g protein

peas and thank you

homestyle chocolate chip cookies with sea salt

Makes 16 to 20 cookies

I ALMOST BROKE UP WITH MY NOW HUSBAND OVER A BATCH OF CHOC-olate chip cookies.

Not long after we started dating, Pea Daddy had invited me to join him to have dinner at a pizza place with his best friends. I was somewhat flattered, even if it went against every feminist bone in my body. I naturally assumed the invitation meant that he thought I was very attractive and wanted to show me off to his guy friends in a very Neanderthal sort of way, dragging me in by my ponytail and saying, "The woman…[grunt]…have salad bar." Of course, it also could have meant that he just really liked me, and that he wanted his friends to get to know me. Nah.

Nevertheless, I was a little nervous and insecure, so I thought I would take some insurance with me, in case maybe they didn't think I was as wonderful as Pea Daddy did. Er, does. Er, used to before he read my description pegging him as a sexist caveman. I planned to bake my famous chocolate chip cookies, based on the very not-secret recipe by a Mr. Nest-lay Toll-house.

I obviously wasn't adhering to *The Rules* of not accepting a dinner date the night of the invitation, and so I had only a few short hours to prepare. The problem was Pea Daddy and I had started hitting the gym together in the afternoon. We'd flirt and spot each other while bench pressing, and overall, it was easily the best part of my day. If I made the cookies, I'd miss the nookie.

homestyle chocolate chip cookies with sea salt (page 205)

I decided to put the ball in Pea Daddy's court, called him, and asked him the question that will forever live in infamy in the Pea household.

"Should I make cookies or should I go work out?"

Every man has those moments when the woman in his life asks him a question with no possible correct answer. Among the questions in that same category are: "Does my butt look big?" "Is she prettier than I am?" and "Do you find my mom attractive?" Perhaps Pea Daddy was showing his lack of experience with women by uttering the words that will forever haunt him:

"You should go to the gym. I reap the benefits of you working out."

Like a good wife, I never let Pea Daddy forget that seemingly innocent remark. I'm already planning on buying a tombstone large enough to etch the inscription: "Here lies Pea Daddy. He said I should go to the gym."

A secure woman would have thought, "Awww…that's sweet. He wants to spend time with me." We have established that I'm not that woman. Instead, those words meant one thing and one thing only: HE THINKS I'M FAT.

The feminist in me awoke like a ferocious she-cat. I immediately hung up, threw my gym shoes in the trash can and baked the best damn chocolate chip cookies I've ever made in my entire life. I handed them over to Pea Daddy's friends with the most sugary sweet smile I could manage, and when Pea Daddy reached for one, I smacked his hand like he was a toddler reaching for a lit stove burner.

Maybe his friends thought I was controlling and insecure. Or maybe they just thought I made some pretty incredible cookies. Either way, they'd be right.

INGREDIENTS

1 cup unbleached all-purpose flour

1 cup whole wheat pastry or white whole wheat flour

2 teaspoons baking powder

½ teaspoon salt

½ cup vegan margarine (i.e., Earth Balance), at room temperature

¼ cup organic brown sugar

¼ cup organic sugar

1 teaspoon pure vanilla extract

½ cup non-dairy or organic milk

½ cup dark chocolate chips

1 teaspoon coarse grind sea salt

DIRECTIONS

1 Preheat oven to 350 degrees.

2 In a large bowl, sift flours, baking powder and salt together. Set aside.

3 Using a stand or electric mixer, cream margarine, sugars, vanilla and milk together.

4 Add dry mixture a little at a time to the wet ingredients, until combined. Fold in chocolate chips.

5 Scoop rounded tablespoons of dough onto an ungreased cookie sheet, spacing an inch apart. The dough will not spread much during baking, so press dough into the flat, cookielike shape and size you'd like your cookie to have. Lightly sprinkle tops of cookies with a few granules of coarse-grind sea salt.

6 Bake for 10 to 13 minutes, or until cookies are set and edges are golden brown. Allow cookies to rest on cookie sheet for 1 minute before transferring them to a cooling rack. Store any remaining cookies in an airtight container.

NUTRITION INFORMATION PER SERVING (for 20 cookies): 108 calories, 4 g total fat, 1 g saturated fat, 0 mg cholesterol, 88 mg sodium, 17 g carbohydrates, 1 g fiber, 2 g protein

pea POINTS

Don't skip the sea salt, even it if seems out of place. While you are at it, make a double batch. Consider yourself warned, these go fast.

sweet endings for sweet peas

almond joy cookie bars

Makes 12 bars

SOMETIMES YOU FEEL LIKE A NUT. SOMETIMES YOU FEEL LIKE YOU'LL need to be committed if someone smears peanut butter on one more piece of furniture. Sometimes you feel like you'd kill for a nap, or rather, someone else's nap. Sometimes you feel like you deserve sixty minutes to call a friend back, write a thank-you note, dust the mantel or freshen up with something besides hand sanitizer and a baby wipe. Sometimes you feel like locking yourself in your closet with a *Cosmo* (and a cosmo), but you'll settle for five minutes with a quirky cookbook and an Almond Joy Cookie Bar. Enjoy. You deserve it.

INGREDIENTS

1 cup whole wheat pastry or white whole wheat flour

½ cup old-fashioned oats

½ cup unsweetened, shredded coconut

½ cup roasted almonds, coarsely chopped

½ cup dark chocolate chips

½ teaspoon baking soda

¾ teaspoon salt

¾ cup organic sugar

½ cup almond butter

½ cup non-dairy or organic milk

½ teaspoon almond extract

½ teaspoon coconut extract

DIRECTIONS

1   Preheat oven to 350 degrees. Spray an 8 × 8-inch baking pan with cooking spray and set aside.

2   In a large bowl, combine flour, oats, coconut, almonds, chocolate chips, baking soda and salt.

3   In a smaller bowl, beat together sugar, almond butter, milk and extracts.

4   Pour wet mixture into the dry ingredients and stir until just combined.

5   Spread batter into your prepared pan and bake for 20 to 25 minutes, or until bars are set and edges are browned. Allow pan to cool before cutting into bars.

NUTRITION INFORMATION PER SERVING: 283 calories, 14 g total fat, 5 g saturated fat, 0 mg cholesterol, 160 mg sodium, 32 g carbohydrates, 3 g fiber, 5 g protein

pea POINTS

I double this batch and bake it in a 13 × 9-inch pan for a few more minutes, as required. For an especially decadent dessert, serve a warm bar with a scoop of dairy-free ice cream or whipped topping.

211

sweet endings for sweet peas

mango cupcakes with coconut cream icing

Makes 12 cupcakes

PEA DADDY ENJOYS ANYTHING WITH A TROPICAL FLAIR: overpriced shirts from Tommy Bahama stores, giant tiki replicas in place of nightstands in our bedroom, and root beer that he has shipped directly from the Big Island (I've run out of breath trying to explain why this is not a sustainable practice, believe me). His fondness, I'm sure, comes from our trip with the girls when they were five months and two years old, respectively. When he hears a ukulele or smells coconut oil, he's instantly transported back to when he skipped down the beach with a curly haired Gigi as she experienced the ocean for the first time. I, on the other hand, am instantly transported to trying to discreetly breastfeed a fussy infant in a picnic shelter at the public beach, while the locals smoke some "organic produce" out of soda cans at the picnic table next to us. Thankfully, Lulu has been weaned for a couple of years, and we can all sit and enjoy a taste of the tropics together, no soda cans involved. Just say "No" to drugs, kids, but "Yes" to these cupcakes.

INGREDIENTS

Mango Cupcakes:

1½ cups whole wheat pastry or white whole wheat flour

2 teaspoons baking powder

½ teaspoon salt

½ teaspoon ground ginger

⅔ cup coconut milk (light or full fat)

1 teaspoon coconut extract

½ teaspoon vanilla extract

⅔ cup organic sugar

⅓ cup orange juice

1 cup diced mango

pea POINTS

Toasting coconut is really simple: just put it in a small dry skillet over medium heat and stir frequently until golden brown. Or you can toast coconut in the microwave to save time. Simply place the coconut in a glass bowl and microwave on high for a minute. Stir and return to microwave in 30-second intervals, stirring after each round, until coconut is golden and aromatic.

Coconut Cream Icing:

½ cup vegan margarine (i.e., Earth Balance)

1¾ cups organic powdered sugar

3 tablespoons coconut milk (light or full fat)

½ teaspoon coconut extract

1 cup toasted, unsweetened coconut

DIRECTIONS

1   For the cupcakes, preheat oven to 350 degrees. Line a muffin tin with cupcake papers.

2   In a large bowl, combine flour, baking powder, salt and ginger.

3   In a separate bowl, combine coconut milk, extracts, sugar and orange juice.

4   Pour wet mixture into dry ingredients and stir until just combined. Fold in mango. Spoon batter into muffin cups.

5   Bake for 18 to 20 minutes, or until a toothpick inserted comes out clean. Allow to cool completely before icing.

6   For the icing, beat margarine for a couple of minutes using an electric mixer. Add in powdered sugar, coconut milk and extract.

7   Frost each cooled cupcake with coconut cream icing and sprinkle with toasted coconut.

NUTRITION INFORMATION PER SERVING: 211 calories, 3 g total fat, 3 g saturated fat, 0 mg cholesterol, 107 mg sodium, 45 g carbohydrates, 1 g fiber, 2 g protein

pb and j–filled cupcakes

Makes 12 cupcakes

MY JEALOUSY OF OTHER WOMEN STARTED AT A YOUNG AGE. IN FIRST grade, I sat next to Rebecca, and oh, how I wanted to be her. It wasn't the fact that she was a clothes horse, though she did have a different outfit every day of the week, and my guess is they most likely covered up those enviable day-of-the-week underwear that she probably wore on the *correct* day of the week. I was in the only clean pair available, which sometimes meant my brother's Star Wars Underoos. My envy also didn't stem from the fact that Rebecca's hair was perfect, though she wore long perfectly woven braids every day, sprouting from a meticulously made part and topped with silky color-coordinated ribbons. My own hair was going through an experimental phase, flip-flopping on whether it wanted to be straight or not. No, fashion and hairstyles aside, I wanted to be Rebecca for one reason and one reason alone: her lunch.

The plain brown bag deceivingly masked the beauty of the objects of my desire, yet the twinges of jealousy started as soon as Rebecca pulled the paper cocoon from her desk. She'd unfold the top, and with each object that emerged, I'd salivate even more.

Clunk.

Down went the entire soda can of Coke. My eyes would dart around the class. Did anyone else see this? Her mom isn't splitting a soda four ways?

Crinkle crinkle.

Out came the "Fun Size" bag of Doritos that was most certainly bought at that mysterious mecca that I'd heard of but had never been to: Costco.

Ffffft.

She'd unzip a Ziploc bag and I'd catch a strong whiff of creamy Skippy and raspberry jam, and watch in disbelief as each crust-free triangle appeared. The only way I was getting my mom to cut the crusts off was if there was mold growing on them.

But the angels would sing from the heavens when the Holy Grail of Sumpter Grade School lunchtime would crest the lunch bag. The foil caught the florescent lighting and blinded me temporarily as a puddle of drool formed on my

peas and thank you

desk. Rebecca would nonchalantly peel back the petals of foil until the single most beautiful dessert I would ever lay eyes on would appear: a perfect cream-filled Hostess Twinkie. I'd never tasted a Twinkie, but I'd watch with delight as Rebecca bit into the soft cake and the sweet, gooey filling. It was magical, and suddenly my Fig Newton seemed horribly inferior.

Now that Gigi is in school, the gloves are coming off. I'm not about to send her to school without a treat that will be the envy of all the girls in her class. What little girl (or adult) wouldn't love finding one of these in her lunch box? As for her underwear, well, let's just say, it's Monday on the calendar, but Friday in her pants.

pea POINTS

You can substitute almond butter, cashew butter or even gourmet flavored peanut butters (i.e., chocolate or white chocolate) for a tempting variation.

INGREDIENTS

Cupcakes:
1¾ cups whole wheat pastry or white whole wheat flour

2 teaspoons baking powder

½ teaspoon salt

1 teaspoon vanilla extract

⅔ cup organic sugar

⅔ cup non-dairy or organic milk

¼ cup natural peanut butter

Filling:
⅓ cup 100 percent fruit preserves (raspberry or strawberry are best)

⅓ cup natural peanut butter

DIRECTIONS

1. Preheat oven to 350 degrees. Line a muffin tin with cupcake papers or spray with cooking spray.

2. In a mixing bowl, combine flour, baking powder and salt.

3. In a smaller bowl, mix vanilla, sugar, milk and ¼ cup peanut butter.

4. Add wet mixture to dry ingredients and stir until just combined.

5. Place a large spoonful of batter in the bottom of each muffin well. Add approximately ½ to 1 teaspoon of preserves and ½ to 1 teaspoon of peanut butter on top of batter, and then an additional teaspoon of cupcake batter on top of the peanut butter and preserves.

6. Bake cupcakes for 20 to 25 minutes, until tops are golden brown.

NUTRITION INFORMATION PER SERVING: 194 calories, 5 g total fat, 1 g saturated fat, 0 mg cholesterol, 183 mg sodium, 32 g carbohydrates, 2 g fiber, 6 g protein

german chocolate cake

Makes 2 9-inch rounds

YOU CAN NEVER BE TOO SPECIFIC WHEN IT COMES TO GIFT REQUESTS.
Whoever invented the concept of wedding registries was a genius; although
this hardly explains how I ended up with a set of Mickey and Minnie salt and
pepper shakers at my wedding shower. I'm not trying to be materialistic or
greedy, but if someone wants to spend $50 on a gift for me, it should be for
something that I want. I assure you that is definitely not Disney crystal. It's even
more aggravating to me when I ask friends or relatives what they want for their
birthday and they say, "Oh, don't get me anything," or even worse, "Just pick
something that looks like 'me.'" Please tell me that's not how Mickey and Minnie
made it into our spice cupboard.

In a practical sense, every year that a child writes out a Christmas list, he
or she is really just submitting a gift registry. Taking that a step further, the
annual visit to Santa Claus is an oral version of said registry; that is, unless your
children are like mine and treat a visit to Santa Claus like we're sending them
to meet an evil clown who has a taste for toddler ballerinas. Yet because of
this odd tradition, by the time Christmas rolls around in our house, we know
exactly what the girls are hoping to find under the tree.

Perhaps we've taken things a little too far in asking our children to express
their birthday wishes, as we now know not only what the girls want for their
birthday, but also where they want to celebrate, what theme that party should
be, and what kind of cake we'll be enjoying. On a recent Saturday, a good six
months in advance of (and with no inciting mention of) her birthday, Pea Daddy
asked Lulu if she would like to go to the carousel, to which she responded, "No,
I want to go to Disneyland for my birthday!" Duly noted.

As far as cake goes in our family, though, it is even more crucial to be
specific as to what kind you would like, or whoever is baking the cake gets to
decide. When it comes to my mom, German chocolate cake is her absolute
favorite, and thus it is almost always what she chooses to make, nut allergies
or coconut disdain be damned. Trying to feign surprise when she announces
that she "made your favorite," carting in the cake in all its German glory is like

trying to pretend you are into the Winnie the Pooh tea towels that are great for polishing crystal.

Though I wasn't surprised when my mom asked that I make a German chocolate cake for her birthday last year, I was surprised when she had a specific gift request.

"I want you to write my obituary," she said matter-of-factly.

I quickly racked my brain to recall any recent doctor's appointments or if she'd suddenly announced a passion for base jumping.

She explained, "I just don't want to be dead when I hear someone saying how they feel about me."

So after much thought and a few drafts, I presented my mother with a framed version of her obituary, which I read, slightly embarrassed, in front of our family who had gathered to celebrate. I turned red. My mother cried. My brother looked down at his Starbucks gift card like it was a bag full of steaming dog excrement.

"Who wants a piece of cake?" I asked.

INGREDIENTS

Chocolate Cake:

2 ½ cups whole wheat pastry or white whole wheat flour

2 cups organic sugar

2 heaping cups unsweetened cocoa powder

2 teaspoons baking soda

1 teaspoon salt

1 cup brewed coffee

1 cup water

½ cup canola oil

2 teaspoons apple cider vinegar

Caramel Pecan Coconut Topping:

¼ cup vegan margarine (i.e., Earth Balance)

2 cups brown sugar

½ cup non-dairy or organic milk

2 tablespoons cornstarch

½ teaspoon agar agar powder (see In the Peas' Pantry [p. xxiii] for details)

⅓ cup toasted unsweetened coconut (see Pea Points p. 214)

2 cups toasted pecans

Chocolate Icing:

½ cup vegan margarine
(i.e., Earth Balance)

2 cups powdered sugar

1 teaspoon vanilla extract

2 tablespoons non-dairy or
organic milk

¼ cup cocoa powder

dash of salt

DIRECTIONS

1 Preheat oven to 350 degrees.

2 Combine the dry ingredients in a large bowl and mix well.

3 In a small bowl, combine the wet ingredients and add to the dry mixture, stirring until just moistened.

4 Place batter in cake pans that have been lightly sprayed with cooking spray. Bake for 30 minutes or until a toothpick inserted comes out clean.

5 For the caramel pecan coconut topping, melt the margarine in a medium saucepan and add the brown sugar and milk.

6 Quickly whisk in the cornstarch and agar agar. Bring to a slow boil and set aside to thicken (you can refrigerate at this point as well to thicken more rapidly).

7 When topping has thickened, stir in toasted coconut and pecans.

8 To make the chocolate icing, beat all ingredients with an electric or stand mixer until fluffy.

9 For layer cakes, frost the sides and middle layer of cakes with chocolate icing and then put caramel topping on top.

NUTRITION INFORMATION PER SERVING (for 10 slices): 334 calories, 18 g total fat,
5 g saturated fat, 0 mg cholesterol, 205 mg sodium, 119 g carbohydrates, 8 g fiber, 8 g protein

pea POINTS

Extra caramel pecan icing makes an incredible topping for non-dairy ice cream or an over-the-top bowl of oatmeal.

sweet endings for sweet peas

banana split remix

Makes 2 to 4 servings

ICE CREAM KILLS.

I'm not talking about the saturated fat, the artificial colors and flavoring, or the harmful preservatives that are in most brands. I'm referring to the actual act of ingesting a scoop of ice cream on a cone. It has the potential to kill you. I should know.

We were not frequent customers of Baskin-Robbins when I was young, but when Mom or Dad said, "Get your coats, we're going for ice cream," we knew that was where we were headed. It's ironic that John Robbins's *Diet for a New America*, in which he explains why he declined becoming heir to the Baskin-Robbins throne for ethical reasons, was one of the first books about veganism I ever read. For an indecisive child like myself, choosing from thirty-one flavors, especially with enigmatic flavor names like Gold Medal Ribbon, Baseball Nut, and Quarterback Crunch, sucked the fun out of the trip. By the age of four, I had discovered that if I found one flavor I liked and stuck with it, I could end the drama of infinite pink taster spoons, frustrated tears, and impatient parents and scoopers. My flavor of choice: Daiquiri Ice.

It was a bizarre choice for a child and an even more bizarre name for an innocent, fruity and delicate sorbet. Were "Last Sip of a Warm Beer" and "Grandpa's Breath" already taken? Regardless that the selection was destined to lead me into a life of debauchery, a kid's-sized scoop of Daiquiri Ice on a sugar cone was my order each and every time.

Though one might think that perhaps cirrhosis or alcohol poisoning would be the threat to my survival at Baskin-Robbins, it was instead the technique by which I ate my frozen treat that almost sent me to my icy grave. Though my mother's motives were pure, or at least an understandable attempt to keep us from slathering cocktail-flavored ice cream all over our OshKosh overalls, she taught us that the best way to eat an ice cream cone was bottom first. We'd greedily lick the frozen mock booze down to the top of the cone and then tilt our heads back, bite off the pointy end with a resounding crunch and start sucking.

One hot summer day during my fifth year of life, I ordered my usual scoop o' Spring Break in Cabo and set off to devour it with a motivation that has been seen only at elite sporting events, like the Superbowl, Wimbledon, the Olympics and the Nathan's Hot Dog Eating Contest. I worked the top of that cone down in record speed, flipped the cone over and got started on the underside. The problem was, when I bit off the bottom of the pointy-tipped cone, I forgot to chew it before I started to suck my frosty O'Douls out, and the tiny point of wafer was sucked down into my esophagus.

I dropped my slimy sugar tube and gasped for air, but to no avail. Luckily, my mom saw what was going on and immediately asked the indifferent, acne-ridden scooper for a cup of water. The kid yawned, motioned his hand to the left and said, "There's a water fountain over there."

I've never been so grateful for my mother's carefully manicured nails in all my life. She stuck her index finger down my throat, her sharp, long red nail acting like a tiny plastic sword going for a martini olive, and plucked the cone from my throat. I gasped for air, cried a few tears and immediately asked for a replacement cone. Make this one a double.

While we don't visit the ice cream parlor nearly as frequently as I did as a child, Gigi and Lulu still enjoy a scoop from time to time. However, we steer clear of the cocktail replicas and we skip the cones altogether. The best sundaes come in a dish anyway, and that could just save your life.

INGREDIENTS

3 bananas, peeled, cut into 2 to 3-inch segments and frozen for at least 4 hours

¼ cup non-dairy or organic milk (if necessary)

agave syrup to taste (optional)

Toppings:
chopped nuts, all-natural sprinkles, soy whipped topping, fresh fruit, vegan cookie crumbles, Magic Topping (see below), et cetera

DIRECTIONS

1 Put frozen bananas in a food processor or blender and turn on high for several minutes. Stop appliance and scoop down sides. Continue blending for several more minutes until mixture has the consistency of soft-serve ice cream. If necessary, add milk, a small amount at a time, until mixture is smooth.

2 Add agave syrup to taste, if desired (if your bananas are overripe, the "ice cream" should be sweet enough without it). Place ice cream in bowls or parfait glasses and add toppings.

Magic Topping:
2 tablespoons natural peanut butter

⅓ cup dark chocolate chips

DIRECTIONS

Put ingredients in a small dish. Microwave for 30 seconds at a time, stirring after each cycle, until just melted. Pour a small amount over banana "ice cream." When allowed to sit for a minute, the topping will harden and form a shell over the "ice cream."

NUTRITION INFORMATION PER SERVING (for 4 servings): 325 calories, 14 g total fat, 4 g saturated fat, 0 mg cholesterol, 70 mg sodium, 35 g carbohydrates, 6 g fiber, 8 g protein

pea
POINTS

Try other varieties of frozen fruit (i.e., strawberries, mango, pineapple, et cetera) for several ice cream flavors in your split, or get really crazy and combine a few fruits for a delicious mix.

carrot cake with "cream cheese" icing

Makes 1 8 × 8-inch cake or 12 cupcakes

HOW GOOD IS THIS CARROT CAKE? GIGI TURNED DOWN CAKES SHAPED like a unicorn, princess carriage and ballet shoes to serve these cupcakes at her fifth birthday party. As if you needed further convincing, my construction workin', meat lovin' uncle asked for seconds. With nearly a whole carrot in each serving, this cake packs in moist flavor and vitamin A, which will only help you see how fabulous this cake truly is. I won't be surprised if we have a repeat performance at Gigi's sixth birthday. I'll make extra this year, Uncle Jeff.

INGREDIENTS

Carrot Cake:

8 to 10 carrots, steamed and pureed to yield approximately 1 cup

⅓ cup vegan margarine (i.e., Earth Balance), softened to room temperature

¼ cup unsweetened applesauce

¼ cup non-dairy or organic milk

½ cup packed organic brown sugar

⅔ cup organic sugar

½ teaspoon vanilla extract

1¼ cup whole wheat pastry or white whole wheat flour

1 teaspoon baking powder

½ teaspoon baking soda

½ teaspoon salt

1 teaspoon cinnamon

½ teaspoon ginger

½ teaspoon nutmeg

½ cup raisins

"Cream Cheese" Icing:

3 tablespoons vegan margarine (i.e., Earth Balance)

4 ounces vegan cream cheese (i.e., Tofutti Better Than Cream Cheese)

2 cups organic powdered sugar

pea POINTS

If there happen to be leftovers, I always store them in the fridge to keep the icing firm. If there happen to be leftovers, congratulations.

DIRECTIONS

1   Preheat oven to 350 degrees.

2   In a large bowl, cream together pureed carrots, margarine, applesauce, milk, sugars and vanilla and beat until smooth.

3   In a smaller bowl, combine flour, baking powder, baking soda, salt and spices. Add a little at a time to the wet mixture until incorporated. Fold in raisins.

4   Spread mixture in an 8 × 8-inch pan that has been sprayed with cooking spray or a muffin tin that has been lined with cupcake papers. Bake for approximately 25 minutes in a pan or 18 to 20 minutes in a muffin tin, or until an inserted toothpick comes out clean. Allow to cool completely.

5   Whip together icing ingredients with a hand mixer. Frost cakes when they are completely cool.

NUTRITION INFORMATION PER SERVING (for 12 cupcakes): 233 calories, 7 g total fat, 2 g saturated fat, 0 mg cholesterol, 264 mg sodium, 55 g carbohydrates, 2 g fiber, 3 g protein

chocolate cherry bread pudding (page 230)

chocolate cherry bread pudding

Makes 6 to 8 servings

MY MOTTO IN LIFE, OR AT LEAST IN CLOSET, PANTRY, REFRIGERATOR and junk drawer cleaning is, "When in doubt, throw it out." Unfortunately, not every member of my family prescribes to this school of thought. In fact, somewhere between Jack Johnson singing to Gigi to "Reduce, Reuse, Recycle," and Dora's Beach Cleanup Adventure, she has seen to it that I shall never throw so much as an empty toilet paper roll away. It's not even as if I'm taking that cardboard cylinder and cramming it in a dolphin's blow hole, I'm simply making a move in the general vicinity of the *recycling bin*, when Captain Planet steps in and says, "No, Mom! I'm going to use that to make something!"

Unfortunately, she's made a lot of "somethings" in the last year at preschool. There is a stack on the edge of our kitchen island comprised of her creations of cooked spaghetti noodles glued to construction paper, Popsicle sticks turned puppets, and toilet paper roll and dried bean bracelets. On average, three new creations are added every day. Inevitably there comes a day each month when the "island turned landfill" starts to topple, and I have to weed through the pile and determine what stays and what goes. I'd like to keep each and every display of my child's creative talents/reincarnation of garbage, but not only does it pose a fire hazard and attract pests, there is simply no room.

Weeding through the pile is like *Sophie's Choice* all over again, especially with the artist herself hovering over me with a disapproving eye, trying to guess which pile will be preserved and which pile will be sent to the evil plastic bin in our garage. Before you peg me as heartless, I'd like to know how many pieces of copier paper with "*idfjdosj dfofjdifj dsojidfisij*" typed on it I am obligated to keep from "Use a Typewriter Day" in Ms. Julie's class. Distraction is key, whether it's, "Here, have an Anytime Cookie," or "Look, someone threw a perfectly good dirty diaper in the trash!" at which point I innocently slip out to the recycling bin to make a deposit.

peas and thank you

Thankfully, I've found a good use for the artwork that hasn't successfully passed on to the other side: I use it to make grocery lists. Since I shop almost as frequently as Gigi "creates," we've got a pretty good system. Just don't be surprised if you find some dried spaghetti noodles in the bottom of my purse. I'm grateful, though, that I've never had to sneak a loaf of stale bread past the Great Protector of Mother Earth. I simply turn it into Pea Daddy's favorite dessert: bread pudding. After all, a big slice of warm comfort food is a lot more useful than a bread crust collage.

INGREDIENTS

4 ounces silken tofu (firm or extra firm)

2½ cups non-dairy or organic milk

½ cup organic sugar

½ teaspoon vanilla extract

½ teaspoon almond extract

1 loaf whole wheat bread, crust removed and cut into 1-inch cubes

½ cup dark chocolate chips

½ cup dried cherries, chopped

DIRECTIONS

1   Preheat oven to 350 degrees. Spray an 8 × 8-inch baking pan with cooking spray and set aside.

2   Combine tofu, milk, sugar and extracts in a food processor and blend until smooth.

3   Pour into a large bowl and add bread cubes, chocolate chips and dried cherries and mix until bread cubes are evenly coated and mixture is uniform.

4   Pour bread mixture into baking pan and bake for an hour. Slice into squares to serve. I like to serve this with an all-natural or non-dairy whipped topping, like Truwhip or Soyatoo, or with soy/coconut milk ice cream.

NUTRITION INFORMATION PER SERVING (for 8 servings): 278 calories, 8 g total fat, 3 g saturated fat, 0 mg cholesterol, 309 mg sodium, 45 g carbohydrates, 5 g fiber, 11 g protein

pea
POINTS

I don't always frown upon eating dessert for breakfast. This "treat" is still full of whole grains and protein and is relatively low in added sugar, a claim that can't be made by many a breakfast cereal.

sweet endings for sweet peas

Makes 12 blondies

THE GRASS IS ALWAYS GREENER: CURLY HAIRED GIRLS WANT STRAIGHT hair, brunettes want to be blond and I want to be Oprah. The beauty of these blondies is that they are the best of both worlds—dense, rich and sweet like a blondie, but with the added touch of a thick fudgy layer of chocolate. They are easy enough to pack in a lunch box, but elegant enough to serve to company…or at least to eat in your yoga pants while watching *Oprah*.

INGREDIENTS

Blondies:

¾ cup natural peanut butter

⅓ cup vegan margarine
(i.e., Earth Balance), softened to
room temperature

½ cup packed organic brown sugar

⅔ cup organic sugar

¼ cup unsweetened applesauce

¼ cup non-dairy or organic milk

½ teaspoon vanilla extract

1¼ cups whole wheat pastry
or white whole wheat flour

1 teaspoon baking powder

½ teaspoon baking soda

½ teaspoon salt

Chocolate Ganache:

¾ cup dark chocolate chips

4 ounces extra firm silken tofu

½ teaspoon vanilla extract

pea POINTS

My girlfriend Deb likes to make a double batch and stick half in the freezer. She swears they never make it to a stage of fully defrosted before she can't resist eating one!

DIRECTIONS

1   Preheat oven to 350 degrees.

2   In a large bowl, cream together peanut butter and margarine. Add in sugars, applesauce, milk and vanilla and beat until fluffy.

3   In a smaller bowl, combine flour, baking powder, baking soda and salt. Add a little at a time to the peanut butter mixture until incorporated.

4   Spread mixture in an 8 × 8-inch pan that has been sprayed with cooking spray. Bake for 20 to 25 minutes, until center is firm and edges are browned.

5   Meanwhile, melt chocolate chips in the microwave or in a double boiler. Using a hand mixer or food processor, cream melted chocolate with tofu and vanilla.

6   Let blondies cool entirely before spreading with the chocolate ganache and cutting into squares. Keep refrigerated.

NUTRITION INFORMATION PER SERVING: 252 calories, 9 g total fat, 3 g saturated fat, 0 mg cholesterol, 173 mg sodium, 40 g carbohydrates, 3 g fiber, 6 g protein

just like bobo's chocolate silk pie

Makes 1 9-inch pie

EVERY FAMILY HAS ITS DESIGNATED PIE MAKER. THIS PERSON MAY HIDE away their dough rolling, edge fluting talents for 363 days of the year, but when Thanksgiving and Christmas come around, it's game time.

My father's mother, "Amah Bobo," was the pie maker for the first twenty-four years of my life. Her unfortunate nickname stemmed from the inability of her grandchildren to pronounce the *gr-* sound combination and from the name of

a cat I'd have a terrible time identifying in a feline lineup. Really though, Amah Bobo should be grateful she got off so easily, as my other grandmother was known only as "Kinky." Try writing that on a birthday card without a snicker.

Ridiculous moniker aside, Bobo could *bake*. She had all the necessary hardware, from Pyrex pie plates and professional rolling pins to all the somewhat unnecessary hardware, such as pie shields and rolling mats that indicated just how far to roll out the precious dough. "Over-rolling," I learned early on in my life, was a sin equivalent to buying a frozen Sara Lee pumpkin "pie" for Thanksgiving.

By most other standards of her life, from her informal education that ended within the eighth grade to her marriage at fifteen, she was what others might call "unsophisticated," yet you'd never guess it by the designer shoes on her feet, the Martha Stewart–esque table settings she created, and the elegant way she carried herself. Her appreciation of the finer things translated into a flawless and delicate crust for whatever filling we were treated to on the occasion at hand.

The pie that I begged her to make each holiday was her Chocolate Mousse Pie with a Chocolate Cookie Crust. Though a quick Google these days can procure just about any recipe an eager cook wishes to find, Bobo liked to hold her "secret recipe" over our heads, and she also refused to make the rich, chocolate dessert on every holiday for fear that it would lose its mystical allure.

Amah Bobo passed in 2004 from lung cancer, a consequence undoubtedly of the cigarettes she'd sometimes enjoy while we smacked our lips and moaned over her creations. One of the important questions the family faced, aside from how we could possibly endure the loss of this lively, generous woman who defined our family, was who would take over the role of the family pie maker? I felt honored to try.

Though this recipe isn't hers, it does embody the flakiness of her crusts, the richness of her chocolate mousse, and her deep appreciation for quality ingredients. I can't help but think she would be proud.

Then she'd remind me not to over-roll the crust.

PIECRUST INGREDIENTS

1¼ cups whole wheat pastry or white whole wheat flour	½ cup cold vegan margarine (i.e., Earth Balance), cut into ½-inch pieces
½ teaspoon organic sugar	
½ teaspoon salt	2 tablespoons to ¼ cup ice water

DIRECTIONS

1 Pulse flour, sugar and salt in a food processor. Add margarine and pulse until mixture forms coarse crumbs, about 10 seconds.

2 With machine running, add ice water in a steady stream until dough holds together without being wet or sticky, no longer than 30 seconds.

3 Shape dough into a flat disc, about the size of a CD. Wrap in plastic and refrigerate for at least an hour before rolling out and putting in a pie pan. Crimp edges using your fingers or a fork.

4 Crust should be blind baked (filled with pie weights or tinfoil and dried beans) at 350 degrees for 18 to 22 minutes, or until golden brown. A pie shield or tinfoil shaped around the rim of the pie plate will prevent over-browning. Cool crust completely before filling.

CHOCOLATE SILK PIE INGREDIENTS

1½ cups quality dark chocolate

2 12-ounce packages silken tofu (firm or extra firm), drained and crumbled

¾ cup non-dairy or organic milk, heated until warm

½ teaspoon vanilla extract

1 prebaked Just Like Bobo's Piecrust, cooled

DIRECTIONS

1 Melt chocolate in a double boiler or in the microwave.

2 Combine chocolate, tofu, heated milk and vanilla in a food processor or blender and blend until completely smooth.

3 Chill mousse until ready to fill cooled crust. Spread filling in crust and chill pie for at least 2 hours or longer before serving. If desired, serve with a non-dairy or all-natural whipped topping, such as Truwhip or Soyatoo.

NUTRITION INFORMATION PER SERVING (for 10 slices): 215 calories, 12 g total fat, 5 g saturated fat, 0 mg cholesterol, 159 mg sodium, 21 g carbohydrates, 4 g fiber, 8 g protein

peas and thank you

lemon raspberry pie (page 240)

lemon raspberry pie

Makes 1 9-inch pie

AT THE RISK OF BEING SEXIST, I'M GOING TO CALL THIS A GIRLY DESSERT.
It's just right for a tea party, Mother's Day, or a certain maternal vegetable's birthday on May 2nd. I like to bring this gorgeous vegan pie to those family gatherings, because really, what's a holiday about if it's not pushing your lifestyle choices on your family? Luckily for me, I've got a roomful of willing victims.

INGREDIENTS

1 prebaked Just Like Bobo's Piecrust (p. 235)

¼ cup plus 2 tablespoons arrowroot powder

1½ tablespoons agar agar powder, (see In the Peas' Pantry [p. xxiii] for details)

1⅓ cups lemon juice

2 cups organic sugar

1 cup non-dairy or organic milk

1 cup water

pinch of salt

zest of 2 lemons

1 pint fresh raspberries

non-dairy or all-natural whipped topping (i.e., Truwhip or Soyatoo) for garnish

DIRECTIONS

1 For the filling, whisk arrowroot, agar agar and lemon juice together in a large saucepan.

2 Once thoroughly combined, add sugar, milk, water and salt and bring slowly to a boil over medium heat, stirring constantly.

3 Once the mixture has come to a slow boil, remove it from the heat. Add the lemon zest and stir well. At this point, you can transfer the filling to a small dish and refrigerate until cool, stirring every once in a while.

4 When both the filling and crust are cool, pour the filling into the crust. Refrigerate pie for at least an hour.

5 Top with fresh raspberries and non-dairy or organic whipped topping, if using, before serving.

NUTRITION INFORMATION PER SERVING (for 10 slices): 259 calories, 2 g total fat, 0 g saturated fat, 0 mg cholesterol, 166 mg sodium, 59 g carbohydrates, 4 g fiber, 4 g protein

pea POINTS

Fresh berries are one of the few fruits that you should never wash too long before using, as they get mushy pretty quickly. If you are making this pie ahead of time, wait to add the raspberries until right before serving…and guard those berries as necessary.

sweet endings for sweet peas

funky monkey pie

Makes 1 9-inch pie

OF ALL THE MARGINALLY IMPRESSIVE ACCOMPLISHMENTS I'VE HAD IN my life, perhaps the one that I am most proud of is my ability to imitate a monkey. Oh yes, I've perfected it to an art form. With my ears pulled out, my upper lip puffed full of air and an uncanny, "Oh oh, eee eee, ah ah ah," I've defused many an escalating meltdown or distracted my kids from a knee scrape.

I'm glad Gigi has my hair and flair for the dramatic. I'm amazed Lulu has my chin and love of books. I'll be downright proud if the girls will someday scratch their armpits, leap around and howl like monkeys. A mother can dream, can't she?

peas and thank you

INGREDIENTS

1 organic store-bought graham cracker crust (i.e., Arrowhead Mills)

1 12-ounce package silken tofu (firm or extra firm)

$\frac{2}{3}$ cup natural peanut butter

$\frac{2}{3}$ cup organic powdered sugar

1 teaspoon vanilla extract

2 tablespoons non-dairy or organic milk (if needed)

2 bananas, sliced

Garnishes:
non-dairy or organic whipped topping (i.e., Truwhip or Soyatoo), chocolate shavings and dry-roasted peanuts

For impatient monkeys, put the pie in the freezer to help it set quickly. Don't worry about leaving it in too long; it tastes great frozen, too!

DIRECTIONS

1 Preheat oven to 375 degrees.

2 Remove crust from packaging and bake for 5 to 7 minutes, or until crust is golden and fragrant. Set aside to cool.

3 While crust is cooling, combine tofu, peanut butter, sugar and vanilla in a blender and blend until smooth. Add milk, if necessary, to get a smoother consistency.

4 Layer sliced bananas in the bottom of the cooled piecrust. Pour peanut butter pudding on top. Refrigerate for at least an hour, or until pie is set.

5 Garnish with whipped topping, chocolate shavings and peanuts.

NUTRITION INFORMATION PER SERVING (for 10 slices): 236 calories, 10 g total fat, 2 g saturated fat, 0 mg cholesterol, 141 mg sodium, 33 g carbohydrates, 2 g fiber, 6 g protein

peanut butter cookie dough balls

Makes 12 cookie dough balls

WHEN I BAKED MY FIRST BATCH OF PEANUT BUTTER COOKIE DOUGH Balls after we wrapped this manuscript, I had no idea that they would even turn out, let alone take the blog world by storm. To date, this is my most popular

recipe ever and I have the marriage proposals to prove it. No cookbook of mine could be complete without what have lovingly become known as "Mama Pea's Balls."

INGREDIENTS

½ cup non-dairy margarine (i.e., Earth Balance)

¾ cup natural peanut butter

½ cup organic brown sugar

¾ cup organic powdered sugar

½ teaspoon vanilla extract

1 teaspoon baking powder

½ teaspoon baking soda

¾ teaspoon salt

1 cup whole wheat pastry or white whole wheat flour

½ cup unbleached organic flour

non-dairy or organic milk (if needed)

½ cup non-dairy chocolate chips

½ cup natural peanut butter chips

DIRECTIONS

1   Using a stand mixer, beat margarine, peanut butter, sugars and vanilla until fully incorporated.

2   In a separate bowl, combine baking powder, baking soda, salt and flours.

3   Add dry mixture to the mixer bowl a little at a time and mix until a dough forms. If dough seems dry, add an additional tablespoon of peanut butter or milk, as needed.

4   Add in chocolate and peanut butter chips. There's no need for exact measurements here. I won't tell.

5   Chill dough for 30 minutes.

6   You could just eat the dough at this point, then send me an email to propose marriage. If you want the full Cookie Dough Ball experience though, preheat oven to 350 degrees. Scoop dough with a mini ice cream scoop (or your fingers) and place balls on a cookie sheet.

7   Bake for 10 to 12 minutes. They'll still be soft and look much like they did going in, but don't overbake. Let the cookie dough balls rest on the pan for a minute before transferring to a cooling rack…if you can wait that long.

NUTRITION INFORMATION PER SERVING: 140 calories, 6 g total fat, 2 g saturated fat, 0 mg cholesterol, 168 mg sodium, 24 g carbohydrates, 2 g fiber, 6 g protein

converting to metrics

volume measurement conversions	
U.S.	METRIC
¼ teaspoon	1.25 ml
½ teaspoon	2.5 ml
¾ teaspoon	3.75 ml
1 teaspoon	5 ml
1 tablespoon	15 ml
¼ cup	62.5 ml
½ cup	125 ml
¾ cup	187.5 ml
1 cup	250 ml

weight measurement conversions	
U.S.	METRIC
1 ounce	28.4 g
8 ounces	227.5 g
16 ounces (1 pound)	455 g

cooking temperature conversions	
CELSIUS/CENTIGRADE	0°C and 100°C are arbitrarily placed at the melting and boiling points of water and standard to the metric system.
FAHRENHEIT	Fahrenheit established 0°F as the stabilized temperature when equal amounts of ice, water and salt are mixed.

To convert temperatures in Fahrenheit to Celsius, use this formula:
$C = (F-32) \times 0.5555$

So, for example, if you are baking at 350°F and want to know that temperature in Celsius, use this calculation: $C = (350-32) \times 0.5555 = 176.65°C$

peas and thank you

index

peas and thank you

peas and thank you

peas and thank you

peas and thank you

about the author

SARAH MATHENY USED TO EAT MEAT AND PRACTICE LAW. AND THEN she became a mom.

A graduate of Linfield College and Willamette University College of Law, Sarah left her life as a family law attorney to raise a family seven years ago, with every intention of returning to a corner office someday.

As a new mom, she made changes to her long-term plan and her family's diet. She started www.peasandthankyou.com to connect with an audience that didn't need to be burped or changed, and to share the joys, successes and laughs that come from raising a mainstream family on non-mainstream meals. Through anecdotes and recipes, Sarah built a following of readers across the country, eager for their daily recipe and/or glimpse into life with the Peas.

And she never looked back.

Sarah lives in Salem, Oregon with her husband, two daughters and a temperamental cat.